作者
歐曼娜

總編輯
黃淑惠

文稿協助
陳寶妃、陳素真
蔣瑞容、蔡壽蓮
徐紹員、何久恩、賴燕貞

攝影
江文榮

電腦排版
大光華印務部

印刷
錦龍印刷實業股份有限公司

味全出版社有限公司
台北市仁愛路四段28號2樓
郵政劃撥00182038號 味全出版社帳戶
電話:(02)2702-1148 . 2702-1149
傳真:(02)2704-2729

版權所有:局版台業字第0179號
中華民國1998年2月初版
1998年4月2版 2-1-4
定價:新台幣參佰元整

Author
Omana Jacob

Chief Editor
Su-Huei Huang

Editorial Staff
Pao-Fei Chen . Su-Jen Chen
Ruth Chiang . Shou-Lien Tsai
Mandy Hsu . John Holt . Yen-Jen Lai

Photography
Williams Chiang

Printed in Taiwan,
Jin-Long Printing Co.Ltd.

WEI-CHUAN PUBLISHING
1455 Monterey Pass Road, #110
Monterey Park,CA 91754, U.S.A.
Tel: 213-261-3880 . 213-261-3878
Fax: 213-261-3299

1ST PRINTING, FEBRUARY 1998
2ND PRINTING, APRIL   1998
ISBN 0-941676-76-5 (Chinese/English)

作者介紹 A Word about Omana Jacob

歐曼娜在小時候觀看祖母煮菜時，就對烹飪這門藝術感到興趣，隨後的三十年間，她更不斷地吸取並鑽研傳統印度料理，以使它更豐盛而多樣化。她曾在印度及台灣兩地有豐富的烹飪教學經驗，這些經驗也使她在設計菜餚時不僅合乎大眾化的口味，且不失印度風味。

歐曼娜也是一位擁有科學和教育學位的專業教師。烹飪對她來說原本僅是娛樂，但現在已成為她十分熱衷的事業。她同時也是一位自由作家，目前和任職英文教授的丈夫一同住在台灣。

Omana became interested in the art of cooking at a very young age when she used to watch her grandmother cook. Over these past three decades, she imbibed the rich and varied traditions of Indian Cooking. She has given many cooking demonstrations in India and Taiwan, and has skillfully adapted the recipes according to the needs of the general users without sacrificing the essential Indian character.

She is a teacher by profession who has degrees in Science and Education. Cooking is her hobby which has now grown into a passion with her. She is also a freelance writer and is currently residing in Taiwan with her husband who is a professor of English.

作者感言 Author's Note

由於本身對烹飪的熱愛及朋友的鼓勵，促使我寫成這本書，主要目的是希望使印度菜餚能行銷世界，廣受大家的喜愛。在眾多的印度菜餚中，基於材料採買的方便性及作法的簡便性，特別選定這100道頗具代表性的佳餚。

我特別要感謝已在國際享有盛名的味全出版社給我的信心，使我的夢想成真。同時我也要感謝 Dora Nein, Amber Wang, Joyce Chang, Kelly Chui 和 Grace Liang 給與我的協助。

最後，我要將這本書獻給我的丈夫Jacob George，女兒Sheena，和兒子Binnu，感謝他們對我努力的事業給與了解及支持。

My endeavors in cooking and the encouragement from my friends prompted me to write this book. The purpose of this book is to acquaint people the world over with Indian cooking. From a wide variety of dishes I have selected these recipes based on the availability of materials and their relative simplicity.

I would like to thank the WEI-CHUAN Publishers who are well established with an international reputation, for having faith in me and making my dream come true. I am grateful to Dora Nein, Amber Wang, Joyce Chang, Kelly Chui and Grace Liang for helping me in this project.

Finally, I dedicate this book to my husband Jacob George, daughter Sheena and son Binnu for their understanding and support in all my endeavors.

目錄

Contents

量器介紹 Conversion Table

1杯（1飯碗）=16大匙
1 cup (1c.)=236c.c.

1大匙（1湯匙）
Tablespoon (1T.)=15c.c.
1斤＝600公克　1兩＝37.5公克

1小匙（1茶匙）
1 teaspoon (1t.) =5c.c.

序對印度菜而言，香料是烹調上不可或缺的材料，就像食物是生命的要素般重要。印度菜從遠古時就以其豐富而辛辣的口味著稱，但現今烹飪已成了一門複雜的藝術，其所注意的焦點不再只是食物的口味，同時也包括營養價值和上菜時的美觀。

印度的主食是米和麥，它們常被做成各種不同式樣與不同配料的組合來食用。印度境內不同的宗教、種族和傳統，造就了寬廣多變而絕妙的素食和非素食菜餚。不同的香料組合，不僅有其特殊的風味，同時也可用來開胃、幫助消化及盤飾。

印度菜每餐均由各種不同的〝羅沙〞(即甜、鹹、辣、澀、酸、苦等味道)組成，再搭配優格或其它沾醬，以調合味覺使風味更佳。如一組四人食用的菜單為：咖哩雞(見52、53頁)、煎魚(見37頁)、咖哩綠豆(見24頁)、青豆馬鈴薯(見35頁)、原味或辣味優格(見11頁)、番茄沙拉(見13頁)及點心，再與米或麥配食。以上範例僅供參考，讀者亦可根據個人喜愛變化菜單。

在家庭的餐宴中，每一道菜皆以公筷母匙的方式供個人取用；只有在某些特殊場合才以套餐形式供應。

此外，在書中每道菜都有註明份量的香料及調味料，但讀者仍可依自己的口味略作調整。

言歸於此，請即刻開始試做這些具特殊風味的菜餚並享受做印度菜的樂趣吧！

Introduction

Food is the essence of life, and for Indians, spices are the essence of food. Indian food has been renowned from time immemorial for its rich and spicy flavor, but cooking today has grown into such a complex art, that considerable attention is paid not only to the rich flavor of the food, but also to its nutritional value and presentation.

Rice and wheat form the staple food in India. They are served in different styles and combinations. India's great diversity of religions, races and traditions have contributed to the creation of a wide variety of exquisite vegetarian and non-vegetarian dishes. Different spice-blends are used for their flavor and also for their appetizing, digestive and decorative qualities.

A typical Indian meal usually includes the following: chicken curry (see pp. 52, 53), fried fish (see p. 37), skinless mung bean curry (see p. 24), peas and potatoes (see p. 35), plain or spicy yogurt (see p. 11), tomato salad (see p. 13) and a dessert along with rice or wheat. This is just an example. However, the readers are free to make their own choices suitable to their taste. This covers many different "Rasas" (sweet, salty, bitter, astringent, sour, pungent, etc.) or flavors of an Indian meal. Yogurt and other dip sauces are served to get a favorable balance of various flavors.

During a family meal, all the dishes are set on the dining table with serving spoons in each of them. When the meal begins, each person helps himself using the spoon to serve food into his plate. On special occasions, a traditional meal is served following a set course.

Though specific measurements of the ingredients are given in each recipe, you may adjust the seasonings according to your taste.

So go ahead and try these exotic and interesting dishes and experience the joy of Indian cooking!

BON APPETIT!

香料介紹

Introducing Spices

印度菜常用的香料均為取自水果、植物的種子及根部、樹皮或灌木皮的天然製品,可用來增加各種菜餚的香味。

香料是印度菜之鑰。印度人常以各種不同的方法大量使用香料,每一道印度菜都會使用不同的香料組合來調味,而這香料組合即稱為這道菜的〝馬撒拉〞或〝咖哩粉〞。想要有好的香味及口感,建議您使用新鮮的香料自己磨粉使用。若要節省時間,可將乾燥的香料如:辣椒、小茴香、小豆蔻、丁香等先磨粉保存於密封瓶中,能使香味持續半年之久。

● 以下所介紹的香料均可在超級市場或中藥店購得。各種印度香料粉,美廚有製售(電話:2596-5221)。

"SPICES" is a general term covering a wide variety of aromatic seasonings which are used to flavor salty and sweet dishes. These are natural products obtained from fruits, seeds, roots, or bark of trees and shrubs.

Spices are the key to Indian cooking. Indians use spices, often lavishly, in many different ways. Each dish has a different combination of spice blends which is called the "Masala" or the curry powder of the dish. To bring out the best flavor and taste, it is advisable to use freshly powdered spices. But to save time, dry spices like pepper, cumin, cardamom and cloves can be powdered in advance and stored in air tight bottles. They can keep their flavor for at least half a year.

● All the spices given below can be found in supermarkets or in Chinese medicine stores.

1 黑胡椒粒　一種取自熱帶植物的小種子,有辛辣味,可整粒或磨粉使用。

2 小豆蔻　一種內部有黑色種子的果實,常用來調製咖哩或加入米食中調味,可整粒敲碎或磨粉使用。

1 **Black pepper corns** Small berries of a tropical plant. Have a hot sharp taste. Used whole or in the powdered form.

2 **Cardamoms** An aromatic pod with dark seeds. Used for flavoring curries, rice preparations etc. Also used in the powdered form.

3

4

5

6

7

8

9

10

3 **肉桂** 帶有刺激味道的紅棕色乾燥樹皮。常以片狀或磨粉使用。

4 **丁香** 一種熱帶植物之花苞乾燥而成，帶有刺鼻香味。可整粒或磨粉使用。

5 **胡荽子** 即為香菜(又名芫荽)的種子，有粒狀及粉狀，是烹製印度咖哩的主要成份。而香菜則可用來調味或裝飾。

6 **小茴香子** 棕色的小種子，常被用來增加咖哩的香味，亦可磨粉使用。

7 **茴香子** 黃棕色的長椎形種子，具怡人香味，可略磨碎或磨粉使用。

8 **印度咖哩粉** 一種常用於咖哩菜餚的綜合調味粉。

9 **芥茉子** 圓形的小種子，有黑色及黃色二種，除用來調味外，芥茉粉用在醃漬物中，亦有保存作用。

10 **豆蔻** 似彈珠大小的堅果，硬且呈深棕色，味道很香，可敲碎或磨粉使用。

3 **Cinnamon** The bark of a tree which has an aromatic flavor. Used as sticks or in the powdered form.

4 **Cloves** Dried buds from a tropical plant. Used whole or ground.

5 **Coriander seeds** Small round seeds, ground and used in almost all curries. Coriander plants commonly known as Chinese parsley; are used for garnishing and flavoring.

6 **Cumin seeds** Small creamish brown seeds. Used in curries to enhance the flavor. The ground powder is also used in some dishes.

7 **Fennel seeds** Small yellowish brown spindle shaped seeds. They have a pleasing flavor. Coarsely powdered seeds are used for seasoning many dishes.

8 **Indian curry powder** A combination of spice powders that are commonly used in curries. Available in small bottles.

9 **Mustard seeds** Tiny round seeds used for seasoning vegetables and meat. Mustard powder is also used in pickling as a preservative.

10 **Nutmeg** Aromatic nut with a hard shell, each one is marble sized with dark brown color. Nutmeg powder is used to flavor many dishes.

11

12

13

14

15

16

17

18

11 八角 是一種中國的香料，種子包含在豆莢內，常用於咖哩菜餚中，或可用來烹調滷味。

12 鬱金香粉 一種深黃色的粉末，少量使用可增添菜餚的色澤與香味。

13 辣椒 有新鮮的紅或青辣椒，成熟的辣椒晒乾即成乾辣椒，乾辣椒又可磨成粗粒或磨成粉儲存，可視菜餚選擇使用。

14 椰子 為熱帶果實，為方便使用，其椰肉常乾燥處理後製成椰子粉或椰奶粉，用於咖哩菜餚中。椰子粉又可自製成椰奶或用市售的椰奶粉泡製（見38頁）。

15 蒜 具特殊香味，常略拍或切碎使用。搗成蒜泥也常被用來醃製肉類。

16 薑 能去腥，磨碎的薑泥可用來醃魚或肉類，薑末或乾薑粉也常用於菜餚的調味。市面上亦有現成的薑粉出售。

17 洋蔥 具特殊香味，可於沙拉中生食或切碎爆香使用於咖哩菜餚或醬汁。洋蔥圈可用作盤飾或調味。較小者可作醃漬物，而洋蔥泥可用來醃肉。

紅蔥頭 類似洋蔥但少辛辣，常整粒或切碎使用於菜餚中增加香味。

18 原味優格 可用於醃肉或作菜餚的咖哩濃汁，亦可調製成各種不同口味的飲料。

11 Star anise Is a dry star-shaped fruit of an evergreen tree native to China. The seeds are contained in the pods. Used in many curries.

12 Turmeric powder A dark yellow powder used in small quantities to impart color and flavor.

13 Chilies A hot flavoring spice. Both red and green chilies are used in many of the Indian curries. The ripe red ones are dried and crushed to make flakes. Fine chili powder is used in curries.

14 Coconut A tropical fruit. Its kernel is dried and made into flakes. Both coconut milk and flakes are used in curry dishes. Cocomilk can be made from coconut flakes. (see p.38.)

15 Garlic Possesses a distinct strong flavor. Used for seasoning in many dishes. Garlic paste is used in marinating meat items.

16 Ginger One of the most important items in Indian cooking, as it has a delightful flavor. Ginger paste is used to marinate fish and meat. Chopped ginger is used for seasoning. Dry ginger powder is used as a flavoring agent.

17 Onions Usually large and round with a thin outer skin. They are eaten raw in salads or chopped and sauted in oil or butter to enhance the flavor of many curry dishes. Onion rings are used for garnishing and to prepare certain sauces. Small varieties are ideal for pickling. Onion paste is used in many meat preparations.

Shallot Though they resemble onions, they are less pungent. Shallots are chopped and used for seasoning certain dishes. In some dishes, they are used whole.

18 Plain Yogurt Used for marinating meat and as a thickening agent in curry.

沾醬及沙拉介紹
Sauces and Salads Introduction

　　印度沾醬濃郁味美，有甜、酸、辣等口味，而沙拉多由蔬、果、香料及優格調製而成。它們皆有開胃及幫助消化的功效，是印度菜中不可或缺的一環。

These complement other items in a main meal. Sauces are usually thick gravies that can be sweet, spicy, or sour. Salads are mostly uncooked preparations made of vegetables, fruits, herbs and yogurt. Both sauces and salads stimulate appetites and aid digestion.

辣椒醬
Chili Sauce (Chili Chutney)

1	辣椒末	2大匙
	洋蔥(切碎)	½杯

2	油	2大匙
	醋	2小匙
	鹽	1小匙

1	2 T. chopped chili
	½ c. chopped onions

2	2 T. oil
	2 t. vinegar
	1 t. salt

1 將 1 料壓碎,再加 2 料拌勻即成。可與白飯配食。

1 Crush 1 together, add 2 and mix. Goes well with plain rice.

香菜醬
Coriander Sauce (Dhanya Chutney)

	香菜	4杯
1	洋蔥(切丁)	2大匙
	薑末	1大匙
	紅辣椒末、鹽	各1小匙
	糖	½小匙
	檸檬汁	1大匙
	水	½杯

	4 c. coriander leaves
1	2 T. chopped onions
	1 T. chopped ginger
	1 t. ea.:chopped red chili, salt
	½ t. sugar
	1 T. lemon juice
	½ c. water

1 將香菜及 1 料用攪拌機攪拌成醬即成。可與各式鹹味點心(見72-77頁)配食。

1 Wash and chop the coriander leaves, add 1 then put in a blender. Grind to form a smooth paste. Goes well with all salty snacks (see pp. 72-77).

甜番茄醬
Sweet Tomato Sauce

	番茄(切碎)	2杯
	芥茉子	½小匙
1	洋蔥(切碎)、糖、醋	各½杯
	水	¼杯
	丁香	4粒
	薑末	1大匙
	鹽	1小匙
	小茴香粉、辣椒粉、肉桂粉	各½小匙

	2 c. chopped tomatoes
	½ t. mustard seeds
1	½ c. ea.: chopped onions, sugar, vinegar
	¼ c. water
	4 cloves
	1 T. chopped ginger
	1 t. salt
	½ t. ea.(powder): cumin, chili, cinnamon

1 番茄加 1 料煮10分鐘至濃稠狀備用。

2 油2大匙燒熱,炒芥茉子至爆裂,加入番茄醬再拌炒1分鐘至均勻即可。可與印度香飯(見14頁)、烤麥餅(見19頁)或炸麥餅(見20頁)等配食。

1 Cook 1 with tomatoes for 10 minutes until thick.

2 Heat 2 T. oil and add mustard seeds. When they sputter, add in the cooked mixture. Stir and cook until well blended for a minute. Goes well with Fragrant Rice (see p.14), Paratha(see p.19), Puris (see p. 20), etc.

薑醬
Ginger Sauce

新鮮嫩薑 ………3兩(115公克)	¼ lb. (115g) fresh tender ginger
① 洋蔥(切碎) …………………½杯 水 ………½杯，蒜末 …1大匙	① ½ c. chopped onions ½ c. water, 1 T. chopped garlic
② 紅糖 ……½杯，醋 ……1大匙 鹽 ……1小匙	② ½ c. brown sugar, 1 T. vinegar 1 t. salt

1 嫩薑切碎，加 ① 料用攪拌機攪勻成泥。

2 油½杯燒熱，炒香薑泥並入 ② 料煮2分鐘至均勻。可與麥麵包或豌豆鹹飯(見15頁)配食。

1 Chop ginger and blend in a food-processor with ① to form a paste.

2 Heat ½ c. oil and fry the paste until fragrant. Add ② and cook for 2 minutes until well blended. Goes well with wheat bread and Pulav (see p. 15).

葡萄乾醬
Raisin Sauce

葡萄乾 ……………………1杯	1 c. raisins
① 乾辣椒(略烤)* ……………1條 蒜末、薑末 …………各1大匙 糖 ……1大匙，鹽 ……½小匙 醋 ………¼杯	① 1 fire-roasted dry red chili* 1 T. ea.(chopped): garlic, ginger 1 T. sugar, ½ t. salt ¼ c. vinegar

1 葡萄乾以熱水1杯浸泡約1小時後，與 ① 料用攪拌機攪碎成泥。

2 將葡萄乾泥加熱3-4分鐘至呈濃稠狀，即可與各式炒飯(見17、18頁)配食。做好的醬可裝入瓷器或玻璃瓶內密封保存。

＊ 乾辣椒直接在火上略烤後風味更佳。

1 Soak the raisins in 1 c. hot water for an hour. Blend raisins and ① in a food-processor.

2 Remove and cook for 3-4 minutes until mixture thickens. Goes well with Biryani (see pp. 17,18). Store in a porcelain or glass jar sealed tightly.

＊ Hold the dry chili with tongs directly over the flame until all the sides are uniformly roasted.

椰子醬
Coconut Sauce
(Coconut Chutney)

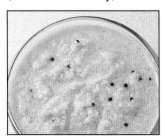

椰子粉 ………………………1杯	1 c. coconut flakes
① 洋蔥泥、薑泥 ………各1大匙 鹽 ………………………1小匙 紅辣椒粉 …………………½小匙 優格 ………………………½杯	① 1 T. ea.: onion paste, ginger paste 1 t. salt ½ t. red chili powder ½ c. yogurt
芥茉子 …………………½小匙	½ t. mustard seeds

1 將椰子粉浸泡在溫水1½杯中半小時，加 ① 料拌勻成醬。

2 油1大匙燒熱，炒芥茉子至爆裂，倒入椰子醬拌勻，冷、熱食皆可。可與綠豆薄餅(見81頁)、綠豆麵球(見83頁)等鹹味點心配食。

1 Soak the coconut flakes in 1½ c. warm water for half an hour. Add ① and mix well.

2 Heat 1 T. oil and add the mustard seeds. When they sputter, add coconut mixture and mix well. Serve hot or cold. Goes well with salty snacks like Mung Bean Pancake (see p. 81), Deep-Fried Mung Bean Balls (see p. 83), etc.

水果醬
Fruit Sauce

酸蘋果或生芒果(去皮，切小
　　丁)* ………… 6兩(225公克)

① 丁香 ……5粒，葡萄乾　2大匙
　蒜末、薑末 ………… 各1大匙
　鹽 ……1小匙，辣椒粉 ½小匙
　糖 ………1杯，醋 ………½杯

½ lb.(225g) finely chopped apples
　or thinly sliced, peeled raw
　mango*

① 5 cloves, 2 T. raisins
　1 T. ea.(chopped): garlic, ginger
　1 t. salt, ½ t. chili powder
　1 c. sugar, ½ c. vinegar

1　將水果及①料放入深鍋中不停攪拌煮10分鐘至濃稠果醬狀，待冷後裝罐保存。可與各式麥餅(見19、20頁)配食。

＊　亦可用蘋果和芒果共6兩(225公克)製成果醬。

1　In a wok, combine the fruit with ① and cook stirring constantly for about 10 minutes until the mixture becomes thick like jam. Cool and preserve in a bottle. Goes well with parathas (see p. 19) and puries (see p. 20).

＊　This sauce can also be made with a total of ½ lb. (225g) of mangoes

辣味優格醬 (一)
Spicy Yogurt I

① 原味優格* ………………1杯
　鹽 ………………½小匙

② 小茴香粉(略烤)** ………1小匙
　辣椒粉 ………………½小匙

① 1 c. plain yogurt*
　½ t. salt

② 1 t. roasted cumin powder**
　½ t. chili powder

1　將①料調勻倒入淺碗中，冷藏1小時，食時撒上②料即成。可與烤麥餅(見19頁)，炸麥餅(見20頁)及素食餃(見72頁)配食。

＊　自製優格：牛奶1杯加原味優格1大匙，置於室溫下約24小時至凝固即成。

＊＊　小茴香子在鍋中乾烤至變色後磨碎。

1　Combine ①, pour into a shallow bowl and chill for an hour. When ready to serve, garnish with ②. Goes well with Paratha (see p.19), Puri (see p. 20) and Samosas (see p. 72).

＊　To prepare yogurt at home: Add 1 T. plain yogurt to 1 c. milk and leave it at room temperature for about 24 hours until set.

＊＊　Dry roast cumin seeds in a frying pan until they change color. Grind into a fine powder.

辣味優格醬(二)
Spicy Yogurt II

① 乾辣椒、蒜瓣 ………各1個

② 洋蔥末、薑末 ………各1大匙

③ 原味優格 ………………1杯
　鹽 ……¾小匙　糖 ……½小匙

　芥茉子 ………………½小匙

① 1 dry red chili and a big clove of garlic

② 1 T. ea.(chopped): onions, ginger

③ 1 c. plain yogurt
　¾ t. salt, ½ t. sugar

　½ t. mustard seeds

1　①料置乾鍋烤至變色取出，加②料攪拌均勻，再加入③料中混合。

2　油1大匙燒熱，炒香芥茉子至爆裂後，倒入優格中拌勻即成。可與米食配食或淋於飯上食用，風味更佳。

1　Fire roast ① until it changes color. Remove and grind with ②. Add to ③ and mix.

2　Heat 1 T. oil and add mustard seeds. When they sputter add to yogurt mixture and combine. Serve with rice.

小黃瓜沙拉
Small Cucumber Salad
(Zucchini Salad)

4人份・Serves 4

	小黃瓜(刨絲)	1杯
	原味優格	1杯
	洋蔥(切丁)	½杯
①	薑末	1大匙
	辣椒末	1小匙
	鹽	½小匙

1 c. shredded small cucumber

	1 c. plain yogurt	
	½ c. chopped onions	
	1 T. chopped ginger	
①	1 t. chopped chilies	
	½ t. salt	

1 將刨絲小黃瓜與 ① 料拌勻後，冷藏食用，可與米飯或麥麵包配食。

1 Combine the shredded cucumber with ① and mix well. Chill and serve with rice or any wheat bread.

蔬菜沙拉
Mixed Vegetable Salad

4人份・Serves 4

	菠菜葉(切碎)	2杯
①	小黃瓜、番茄(均切丁)	各1杯
	香菜(切段)	½杯
	鹽	½小匙
	優格	1杯
	小茴香粉(略烤)	1小匙

	2 c. finely chopped spinach leaves
①	1 c. ea.(chopped): small cucumber, tomatoes
	½ c. chopped coriander leaves, ½ t. salt
	1 c. yogurt
	1 t. roasted cumin powder

1 將 ① 料混合排於淺盤中，倒入優格，並撒上小茴香粉即成，可與米飯或麥麵包配食。

1 Combine ① and arrange in a shallow plate. Pour yogurt over this and garnish with cumin powder. Serve with rice or any wheat bread.

酸味水果沙拉
Tangy Fruit Salad

4人份・Serves 4

	熟香蕉(切片)	1杯
*	鳳梨(切塊)	1杯
①	蘋果(去籽,切片)	1個
	柳橙(剝片)	1個
	葡萄、櫻桃或草莓	各4顆
②	檸檬汁	1大匙
	鹽、胡椒粉	各½小匙

	1 c. sliced ripe bananas
	1 c. chopped pineapple
*	1 apple cored and sliced
①	1 orange segmented
	4 ea.: grapes, cherries or strawberries
②	1 T. lemon juice
	½ t. ea.:salt, pepper powder

1 將 ① 料排盤後淋上 ② 料，冷藏食用。

* 可選用任何水果。最後亦可撒上烤過之小茴香粉以增風味。

1 Arrange ① in a platter,add ②, chill and serve.

* Any kind of fruit can be used in this. You may even add a bit of roasted cumin powder for a different flavor.

馬鈴薯沙拉
Potato Salad

4人份 · Serves 4

	熟馬鈴薯 ········4兩(150公克)			⅓ lb.(150g) boiled potatoes
①	芥茉子、小茴香子、胡椒粒 ············各½小匙		①	½ t. ea.:mustard seeds, cumin seeds, pepper seeds
②	洋蔥(切碎) ·············½杯 紅辣椒末 ·············1小匙		②	½ c. chopped onions 1 t. chopped red chili
③	優格 ·············1½杯 鹽 ·············½小匙		③	1½ c. yogurt ½ t. salt

1　熟馬鈴薯去皮切1公分丁備用。

2　油1大匙燒熱，炒香 ① 料至爆裂，入馬鈴薯丁及 ② 料炒至微黃，倒入 ③ 料中拌勻，冷藏食用，可與米飯或麥麵包配食。

1　Peel and cut the boiled potatoes to ½" (1cm) squares.

2　Heat 1 T. oil and add ①. When they sputter add the potatoes and ②. Saute until they turn slightly brown. Remove and add to ③; mix well, chill and serve. Goes well with rice and wheat bread.

番茄沙拉
Tomato Salad

4人份 · Serves 4

	番茄(切丁)·············1杯			1 c. chopped tomatoes
①	洋蔥末 ·············1杯 檸檬汁 ·············1大匙 薑末 ·············1大匙 紅辣椒末 ·············1小匙 鹽 ·············1小匙		①	1 c. chopped onions 1 T. lemon juice 1 T. chopped ginger 1 t. chopped red chili 1 t. salt

1　番茄與 ① 料拌勻，排於盤上，置冰箱冷藏後食用。與麥麵包配食佳。

1　Combine tomatoes and ① together. Arrange in a plate. Chill and serve. Goes well with wheat bread.

洋蔥優格沙拉
Onion Yogurt Salad

4人份 · Serves 4

	洋蔥(切環狀)* ·············1杯 番茄(切成6塊) ·············1個			1 c. onion rings* 1 tomato cut into 6 pieces
①	優格 ·············1杯 鹽 ·············½小匙		①	1 c. yogurt ½ t. salt

1　將切好的洋蔥排盤，淋上混勻的 ① 料，並用番茄裝飾即成。

＊　洋蔥生食較辛辣，可先加少許鹽，使用前擠乾水份。

1　Arrange the onion rings in a plate. Combine ① and pour over the rings. Decorate with tomato pieces.

＊　To avoid the strong flavor, you may sweat onions with a pinch of salt and squeeze before use.

印度香飯
Fragrant Rice

長粒米(圖1)* ············1 $\frac{1}{2}$ 杯

① 小豆蔻、丁香(均敲碎) 各4粒
奶油 ···················3大匙
肉桂片 ················2 $\frac{1}{2}$ 公分
小茴香子、鹽 ········各1小匙
胡椒粒 ··················$\frac{1}{2}$ 小匙

腰果 ·······················8粒
洋蔥(切片) ··············1杯

1 $\frac{1}{2}$ c. long grained rice (Fig.1)*

① 4 ea. (crushed):
cardamoms, cloves
3 T. butter
1"(2 $\frac{1}{2}$cm) piece cinnamon
1 t. ea.: cumin seeds, salt
$\frac{1}{2}$ t. pepper corns

8 cashew nuts
1 c. sliced onions

1 米洗淨瀝乾後，加 ① 料及水2 $\frac{1}{2}$ 杯入電鍋中煮熟。

2 油3大匙燒熱，分別炒腰果和洋蔥至微黃後撒在飯上作裝飾，可與沙拉(見12頁)或優格醬(見11頁)配食。

* 印度長粒米煮後鬆而不沾黏，若無則以其它米代替。

1 Wash and drain rice. Combine with ① and cook with 2 $\frac{1}{2}$ c.water in a rice-cooker.

2 Heat 3 T. oil, fry cashew nuts and onions separately until slightly brown. Granish them on the cooked rice. Serve with a salad (see p. 12) or a yogurt sauce (see p. 11).

* Indian long grained rice called Basmati is cooked to become soft but not sticky. If not available, other varieties of rice may be used.

1

豌豆鹹飯
Rice and Peas (Mutter Pulav)

長粒米……………………1½杯
新鮮豌豆…………………1½杯
奶油 ………………………3大匙

①
黑胡椒粒、丁香 ………各6粒
小豆蔻(敲碎) ……………3粒
肉桂片………………2½公分
小茴香子 ………………1小匙

洋蔥(切薄片) …………1杯

②
蒜泥、薑泥 ………各½大匙
鹽………………………1小匙
鬱金香粉 …………………¼小匙

1½ c. long grained rice
1½ c. fresh peas
3 T. butter

①
6 ea.: black pepper corns,
   cloves
3 crushed cardamoms
1" (2½ cm) piece of
   cinnamon
1 t. cumin seeds

1 c. thinly sliced onions

②
½ T. ea.: garlic paste,
   ginger paste
1 t. salt
¼ t. turmeric powder

1 米洗淨瀝乾，加水3杯浸泡1小時。

2 奶油燒熱，略炒 ① 料，加洋蔥炒至呈微黃。續入 ② 料炒香後，加豌豆拌炒，再加浸泡過的米及水一起拌勻，入電鍋煮熟(飯熟立即掀開蓋子透氣，並略翻拌)即成。趁熱與冷藏的辣味優格醬(見11頁)或薑醬(見10頁)配食。

1 Wash and drain rice; soak in **3** c. water for an hour.

2 Heat the butter and saute ①. Add onions and stir until slightly brown. Add ② and fry until fragrant. Add peas and mix well. Combine with rice and water. Transfer to a rice cooker and cook until done. Serve hot with chilled spicy yogurt (see p.11) or ginger sauce (see p.10).

蔬菜雜炊
Vegetable Fried Rice

長粒米·····················1 1/2 杯

1 馬鈴薯、花菜、四季豆(均切丁)、豌豆 ········共2 1/2 杯

奶油或瑪琪琳 ···········3大匙

2 洋蔥(切薄片) ···········1杯
丁香粒、胡椒粒(均敲碎) ······
·····················各4粒
小豆蔻(敲碎) ············2粒
肉桂片····················2 1/2 公分

3 薑末、蒜末 ···········各1大匙

番茄(切丁) ·················1杯

1 1/2 c. long grained rice

1 2 1/2 c. mixed vegetables (cut into 1/2 " cubes): potatoes, cauliflower, French beans and peas

3 T. butter or margarine

2 1 c. thinly sliced onions
4 ea.(crushed): cloves, pepper corns
2 crushed cardamoms
1" (2 1/2cm) piece of cinnamon

3 1 T. ea.(chopped): garlic, ginger

1 c. chopped tomatoes

1 將米洗淨瀝乾備用。

2 奶油或瑪琪琳燒熱,炒香 2 料,隨入 3 料炒勻。再放入米及 1 料拌勻後加番茄丁,隨入電鍋中,加鹽1小匙和熱水3杯煮熟即成。可趁熱與辣味優格(見11頁)配食。

1 Wash and drain rice, set aside.

2 Heat butter or margarine and saute 2 until fragrant. Add 3 and fry. Add 1 and stir well, then add tomatoes. Transfer to a rice cooker with 1 t. salt and 3 c. hot water and cook until done. Serve hot with a cup of spicy yogurt (see p. 11).

肉末香飯

Rice and Minced Meat (Keema Biryani)

瘦絞肉 ············6兩(225公克)
長粒米·················1 ½ 杯
奶油 ····················.4大匙

1
洋蔥(切薄片) ··············½ 杯
小豆蔻、丁香(均敲碎) 各4粒
肉桂片·················2 ½ 公分

2
洋蔥(切丁) ··············½ 杯
薑末、蒜末 ··········各1大匙

3
辣椒粉、小茴香粉、胡荽粉
··················各1小匙
豆蔻粉、鬱金香粉、胡椒粉
··················各 ¼ 小匙

4
番茄(切丁) ················1杯
水 ···················½ 杯
鹽 ···················½ 小匙

5
茴香粉 ·················1小匙
肉桂粉 ·················½ 小匙
香菜末 ·················½ 杯

½ lb. (225g) minced lean
  meat
1 ½ c. long grained rice
4 T. butter

1
½ c. sliced onions
4 ea.(crushed):
  cardamoms, cloves
1"(2 ½cm) piece of
  cinnamon

2
½ c. chopped onions
1 T. ea. (chopped): ginger,
  garlic

3
1 t. ea.(powder): chili,
  cumin, coriander
¼ t. ea.(powder): nutmeg,
  turmeric, pepper

4
1 c. chopped tomatoes
½ c. water
½ t. salt

5
1 t. fennel powder
½ t. cinnamon powder
½ c. chopped coriander
  leaves

1 米洗淨瀝乾。奶油2大匙燒熱,炒香 ① 料。加入米拌勻後，隨入電鍋中以熱水2½杯及鹽1小匙煮熟。

2 奶油2大匙燒熱,炒香 ② 料。火轉小，入 ③ 料炒勻，並加絞肉拌炒，隨入 ④ 料以小火煮至汁收乾。撒上 ⑤ 料拌勻即成肉料。

3 碗中塗上奶油，先鋪上一半的肉，再鋪上一半的飯輕壓(圖1)，重複一次將餘料鋪完，置旁5分鐘備用。

4 先用刀沿碗緣切開，再將飯倒扣在盤中(圖2)，趁熱食用。

□ 絞肉可使用任何瘦肉。最後上菜前可以檸檬片或番茄片裝飾。

1 Wash and drain rice. Heat 2 T. butter and fry ① until fragrant. Add rice and mix. Transfer to a rice cooker with 2 ½c. hot water and 1 t. salt. Cook until done.

2 Heat 2 T. butter and saute ② until fragrant. Lower heat; add ③ and stir. Add meat and stir. Add ④, cook over low heat until well done and dry. Add ⑤ and mix.

3 In a buttered bowl arrange ½ of the cooked meat and press lightly. Spread ½ of the cooked rice over the meat (Fig.1). Repeat to form alternating layers of rice and meat. Wait for 5 minutes to set.

4 Invert the bowl into a plate (Fig.2) and serve hot.

□ Any kind of meat can be used in this recipe. You may garnish with lemon and tomato wedges, before serving.

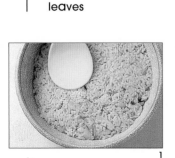
1

2

辣味雞飯

Spicy Chicken Rice (Chicken Biryani)

雞肉塊(去皮)　12兩(450公克)
長粒米·················1 1/2 杯
奶油·················3大匙

[1]
丁香·················6粒
小荳蔻(敲碎)···········5粒
肉桂·················2 1/2 公分
胡椒粒···············1/2 小匙

[2]
鹽、鬱金香粉·····各1/2 小匙
水·················2 1/2 杯

[3]
洋蔥(切碎)···········1杯
薑末、蒜末·········各2大匙
紅辣椒末·············1小匙
香菜末、優格·······各1/2 杯
檸檬汁···············1大匙

[4]
辣椒粉、茴香粉、胡荽粉、
　肉桂粉、鹽·······各1小匙
小茴香粉············3/4 小匙
鬱金香粉············1/2 小匙

[5]
水·················1 1/2 杯
番茄(切丁)···········1杯

水煮蛋(切半)·········2個

1 米洗淨瀝乾。奶油燒熱炒香 [1] 料，加米拌勻，再加 [2] 料以電鍋煮熟。

2 將 [3] 料先以攪拌機攪拌後，加入 [4] 料混合並拌入雞塊醃15分鐘。再加 [5] 料以中火蓋鍋煮15-20 分鐘至雞肉熟軟且汁變濃稠。

3 將雞肉塊與飯混合並以水煮蛋裝飾即成。

---

1 lb. (450g) skinless
   chicken pieces
1 1/2 c. long grained rice
3 T. butter

[1]
6 cloves
5 crushed cardamoms
1" (2 1/2 cm) piece
   cinnamon
1/2 t. pepper corns

[2]
1/2 t. ea.: salt, turmeric
   powder
2 1/2 c. water

[3]
1 c. chopped onions
2 T. ea.(chopped):ginger,
   garlic
1 t. chopped red chilies
1/2 c. ea.: chopped
   coriander leaves, yogurt
1 T. lemon juice

[4]
1 t. ea.(powder): chili,
   fennel, coriander,
   cinnamon, salt
3/4 t. cumin powder
1/2 t. turmeric powder

[5]
1 1/2 c. water
1 c. chopped tomatoes

2 hard boiled eggs (cut in
   half)

1 Wash and drain the rice. Heat the butter and add [1]; stir until fragrant. Add the rice and stir. Add [2] and cook in a rice cooker until done.

2 Combine [3] and blend in a food-processor. Add [4] and mix. Marinate the chicken in this mixture for **15** minutes. Add [5] and cook covered over medium heat for **15-20** minutes until done and a thick gravy is formed.

3 Combine the cooked meat with rice and garnish with hard boiled eggs.

烤麥餅
Roasted Indian Wheat Bread (paratha)

麥粉(圖1) ·············2 1/4 杯
鹽·················1/3小匙
奶油(融化) ··········6大匙
水 ················3/4 杯

2 1/4 c. wheat flour (Fig.1)
1/3 t. salt
6 T. melted butter (Total)
3/4 c. water

1 將篩過之麥粉與鹽拌勻後，加融化的奶油2大匙和水揉成麵糰，置旁約1小時。

2 將麵糰分成8份，並分別趕成0.3公分厚之圓餅，在圓餅上塗奶油後對折，再塗奶油後再對折趕平成三角形(圖2)或任何形狀。

3 將麵餅放入平底鍋內以小火乾烘，並在兩面塗上奶油烘至酥脆且呈微黃色即成。趁熱與各式咖哩配食。

1 Combine the flour and salt; mix well. Add **2 T.** melted butter and knead well with water to make a smooth dough. Set aside for an hour.

2 Divide the dough into **8** balls and roll out each ball into a flat thin disk, 1/8"(0.3cm) thick. Brush butter on this and fold in half. Brush butter again and fold over to form a triangular shape (Fig.2). Roll out the dough to make it thin, maintaining the triangular shape. Any other shape is just as good.

3 Transfer this layered dough to a hot skillet. Cook over low heat, smearing butter on both sides until it becomes flaky and slightly brown. Serve hot with any curry.

1

2

炸麥餅
4人份 · Serves 4
Deep-Fried Indian Wheat Bread (Puris)

麥粉 ······························2杯
鹽 ·····························⅓小匙
水 ·····························½杯

2 c. wheat flour
⅓ t. salt
½ c. water

1 將篩過之麥粉加鹽,並緩緩將水倒入揉成麵糰,可視需要再加少許水。

2 將麵糰分成15個小球,並分別趕成直徑8-10公分之圓餅。

3 油2杯燒熱,將圓餅一次一個以中火炸(稍壓使浸於油中)至鼓起且兩面微黃即成,趁熱與咖哩或葡萄乾醬(見10頁)配食。

1 Mix the salt into the flour. Add water a little at a time, kneading well to form a firm dough. A few drops of extra water may be added if needed.

2 Divide the dough into **15** smooth balls. Roll out each ball into a thin disk of **3"-4"** (**8-10cm**) in diameter.

3 Heat **2 c.**oil and deep-fry the disks one by one over medium heat until they are puffed up and golden brown. Serve hot with any curry or Raisin Sauce (see p. 10).

炸麵餅
4人份 · Serves 4
Deep-Fried Flour Bread (Batura)

① ┌ 酵母(圖1)、糖 ·········各1小匙
  └ 溫水 ·····························¼杯

  ┌ 麵粉 ·····························2½杯
  └ 鹽、小蘇打粉 ·········各½小匙

② ┌ 優格、水 ·············各2大匙
  │ 奶油 ·····························1大匙
  └ 蛋黃 ·····························1個

① ┌ 1 t. ea.: yeast (Fig.1), sugar
  └ ¼ c. warm water

  2 ½ c. flour
  ½ t. ea.: salt, baking soda

② ┌ 2 T. ea.: yogurt, water
  │ 1 T. butter
  └ 1 egg yolk

1

1 ① 料混勻,置旁待起泡備用。

2 麵粉於乾鍋炒熱後與鹽、小蘇打粉混合,再與酵母液拌勻並加②料揉成麵糰,蓋上濕布置於溫暖的地方約3小時。

3 將麵糰分成10份,並分別趕成圓餅,炸熟即成。炸法參考炸麥餅。

1 Combine ① . Set aside until mixture becomes frothy.

2 Warm the flour in a dry pan and mix salt and baking soda together. Add the yeast mixture and ② to the flour mixture. Knead well to prepare the dough. Cover with a wet cloth and set aside for **3** hours in a warm place.

3 Make **10** Baturas like "Deep-Fried Indian Wheat Bread" (Puris).

蔬菜麥餅

4人份 · Serves 4

Vegetable Stuffed Wheat Bread (Stuffed Paratha)

麥粉 ························2 ⅓ 杯
芥茉子 ··················½ 小匙

1 | 洋蔥(切丁) ···············2大匙
  | 薑末 ························1大匙

印度咖哩粉 ··············1大匙

2 | 熟馬鈴薯泥(圖1) ················
  | ·······················6兩(225公克)
  | 辣椒粉、鹽 ·········各½ 小匙

奶油(融化) ··················½ 杯

2 ⅓ c. wheat flour
½ t. mustard seeds

1 | 2 T. chopped onions
  | 1 T. chopped ginger

1 T. Indian curry powder

2 | ½ lb. (225g) boiled mashed potatoes (Fig.1)
  | ½ t. ea.: chili powder, salt

½ c. melted butter

1 將篩過之麥粉加水 ¾ 杯揉成麵糰備用。

2 油2大匙燒熱，炒芥茉子至爆裂，加 1 料炒香，入咖哩粉拌勻，再加 2 料炒勻取出即為餡。

3 將麵糰分成8份，取一份趕成直徑8公分之圓餅。每張麵餅放入 ⅛ 份餡(圖2)後，將邊緣包起再趕平成圓薄餅(圖3)，做時先舖麵粉以防沾黏。

4 奶油2小匙燒熱，放入一個圓餅以中火烤至兩面呈金黃色即成，餘料依此法做完。趁熱與沙拉或優格配食。

1 Prepare a soft dough using the wheat flour and ¾ c. water. Set aside.

2 Heat 2 T. oil and add the mustard seeds. When they sputter add 1 and fry until fragrant. Add the curry powder; mix well. Add 2, mix thoroughly and remove from heat.

3 Divide the dough to make 8 portions. Make a disk 3" (8cm) in diameter with each portion. Put ⅛ of the potato mixture in the middle (Fig. 2), and roll up the sides, and completely cover the mixture. Then flatten and roll out each one to make a thin disk (Fig. 3). Use flour on the board to avoid sticking.

4 Roast over medium heat on a hot skillet with 2 t. butter for each one until both sides turn golden brown. Serve hot with salad or yogurt.

1

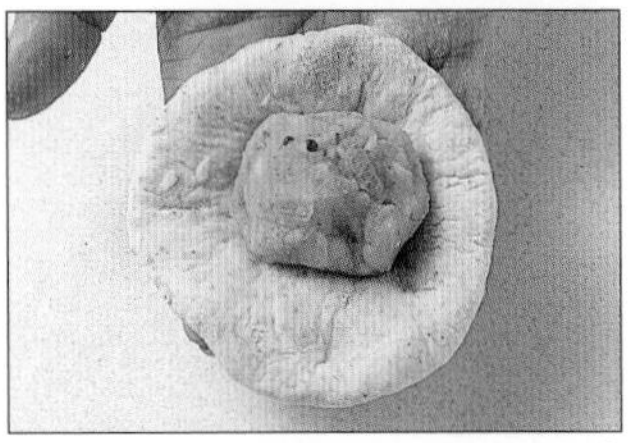
2

3

硬麵包

Baked Flour Bread (Naan)

1 糖、酵母 ………………各1小匙
  溫水 …………………… 1/4 杯

2 麵粉 ……………………… 2 1/2 杯
  鹽、泡打粉 ………各 1/2 小匙
  優格 …………………… 1/4 杯

  黑芝麻 ………………… 1/4 杯
  奶油(融化) ……………… 適量

1 1 t. ea.: sugar, yeast
  1/4 c. warm water

2 2 1/2 c. flour
  1/2 t. ea.: salt, baking
    powder
  1/4 c. yogurt

  1/4 c. black sesame seeds
    melted butter for greasing

1 ① 料混勻待起泡後備用。混合 ② 料並加入酵母液,再邊加水 1/4 杯揉成麵糰。揉麵時,手沾奶油以防粘手,加蓋置旁約3-4小時使膨脹約2倍大。

2 將膨脹之麵糰再揉約1分鐘後分成4份,分別趕成長15-18公分的胡瓜形麵餅,在兩面沾上芝麻,並稍壓入麵糰中使不易掉落(圖1)。

3 將薄餅放入450°F(230°C)的烤箱中烤8-10分鐘至呈微黃色即成。

□ 烤前在烤盤上先抹奶油,或以熱鐵板乾煎亦可。

1 Combine ①. Set aside for the mixture to become frothy. Mix ② and add the yeast mixture. Knead, adding 1/4 c. water to form a dough. Grease palms with butter to avoid sticking. Keep the prepared dough covered for about 3-4 hours until it doubles in size.

2 Knead again for a minute and divide into 4 portions. Shape each portion into a teardrop shape about 6"-7" (15cm-18cm). Spread some sesame seeds on both sides, pressing them into the dough (Fig. 1).

3 Bake in preheated oven at 450°F (230°C) for about 8-10 minutes until it changes to a light brown color.

□ Smear the tray with butter before baking. It can also be roasted on hot griddle.

1

咖哩花豆

Kidney Bean Curry (Rajma Curry)

花豆(圖1) ⋯⋯⋯⋯⋯⋯1杯

1
| 番茄(切丁) ⋯⋯⋯⋯⋯⋯1杯
| 八角 ⋯⋯⋯⋯⋯⋯⋯⋯1粒
| 小蘇打粉 ⋯⋯⋯⋯⋯½小匙
| 水 ⋯⋯⋯⋯⋯⋯⋯⋯5杯

洋蔥(切丁)⋯⋯⋯⋯⋯½杯
蒜泥、薑泥 ⋯⋯⋯各½大匙

2
| 胡荽粉 ⋯⋯⋯⋯⋯⋯1大匙
| 茴香粉 ⋯⋯⋯⋯⋯⋯1小匙
| 辣椒粉 ⋯⋯⋯⋯⋯½小匙

3
| 香菜末 ⋯⋯⋯⋯⋯⋯½杯
| 肉桂粉 ⋯⋯⋯⋯⋯½小匙

1 c. kidney beans(Fig.1)

1
| 1 c. chopped tomatoes
| 1 star anise
| ½ t. baking soda
| 5 c. water

½ c. chopped onions
½ T. ea.(paste): garlic,
    ginger

2
| 1 T. coriander powder
| 1 t. fennel powder
| ½ t. chili powder

3
| ½ c. chopped coriander
| leaves
| ½ t. cinnamon powder

1　花豆浸泡過夜後洗淨瀝乾，與 1 料同煮約40分鐘至汁收乾且花豆熟軟。若煮40分鐘仍未熟透，則再加熱水1杯煮至熟軟。

2　油2大匙燒熱，炒香洋蔥至微黃，再加蒜、薑泥炒香，火轉小，入 2 料拌勻並加花豆、鹽1小匙及水1杯煮約3分鐘後，撒上 3 料混合拌勻即成，趁熱食用。

1 Soak the kidney beans overnight; wash and drain. Cook with 1 for about **40** minutes until they are soft. If the beans are not well cooked even after **40** minutes, add **1** c. hot water and cook until done.

2 Heat **2** T. oil and fry the onions until they are light brown. Add the garlic-ginger paste and fry until fragrant. Lower heat, add 2 and mix well. Add the cooked beans, **1** t. salt and **1** c. water. Simmer for about **3** minutes until well blended. Add 3; mix and serve hot.

1

咖哩綠豆

Skinless Mung Bean Curry (Mung Dal)

綠豆仁(圖1)* ⋯⋯⋯⋯⋯³⁄₄ 杯

① 洋蔥(切丁)、薑末 ⋯各1大匙

② 乾辣椒(切半) ⋯⋯⋯⋯⋯1條
　 小茴香子、芥茉子 ⋯各1小匙

③ 鹽 ⋯⋯⋯⋯⋯⋯⋯⋯⋯1小匙
　 辣椒粉、小茴香粉⋯各³⁄₄小匙

³⁄₄ c. skinless mung bean
(Fig.1)*

① 1 T. ea.(chopped): onions,
ginger

② 1 dry red chili cut into 2
pieces
1 t. ea.: cumin seeds,
mustard seeds

③ 1 t. salt
³⁄₄ t. ea.(powder): chili,
cumin

1　綠豆仁洗淨並泡水2小時。

2　將水瀝乾,加 ① 料及水3杯以中火煮20分鐘至熟軟。

3　油2大匙燒熱,入 ② 料炒至爆裂,火轉小,入 ③ 料拌炒隨即加入煮好之
綠豆仁拌勻,最後撒上香菜末趁熱食用。可與米食或麥麵包配食。

＊　綠豆仁在一般超市均有售。

1　Wash and soak the mung beans for 2 hours.

2　Discard the soaked water, cook with ① and 3 c. water over
medium heat for about 20 minutes until soft and well cooked.

3　Heat 2 T. oil and add ②. When they sputter, lower heat and add
③; mix. Then add to the cooked mung bean immediately. Mix
well and serve hot with chopped coriander leaves. Goes well
with rice or any wheat bread.

＊　Skinless mung beans may be purchased in supermarkets.

1

馬鈴薯炒菠菜
Potatoes and Spinach (Alu Palak)

馬鈴薯(切小丁) 6兩(225公克)
菠菜(切碎) ……6兩(225公克)

☐1
黑胡椒粒(敲碎) ………5粒
小豆蔻(敲碎) …………2粒
辣椒末 ……………1小匙

洋蔥(切碎)……………½杯
蒜泥、薑泥 ……各½大匙

☐2
胡荽粉、小茴香粉、茴香粉…
……………各1小匙

½ lb.(225g) potatoes, cut in
½" (1cm) cubes
½ lb.(225g) chopped
spinach

☐1
5 black pepper corns
(crushed)
2 crushed cardamoms
1 t. chopped chili

½ c. chopped onions
½ T. ea.:garlic paste,
ginger paste

☐2
1 t. ea. (powder):
coriander, cumin, fennel

1 油4大匙燒熱,炒香 ☐1 料並加洋蔥炒至微黃。續入蒜、薑泥炒香。

2 火轉小,入 ☐2 料、馬鈴薯拌炒1分鐘至均勻後加水 ½ 杯及鹽 ½ 小匙,蓋鍋以中火煮3-4分鐘(煮時攪拌1-2次)。

3 倒入菠菜拌炒均勻並煮至汁收乾即成。

1 Heat 4 T. oil and saute ☐1. Add onions and stir until slightly brown. Add garlic-ginger paste and fry until fragrant.

2 Lower heat, add ☐2 and potatoes and stir fry for a minute. Add ½ c. water and ½ t. salt. Cook covered over medium heat for 3-4 minutes, stirring once or twice while cooking.

3 Add spinach, mix and cook until dry.

椰香菜豆

String Beans and Coconut

新鮮菜豆 ………6兩(225公克)

1. 洋蔥(切丁) …………1大匙
   鹽 …………………1小匙
   紅辣椒(剖半) …………1條
   小茴香粉、鬱金香粉 各½小匙

2. 芥茉子、小茴香子…各½小匙

   紅蔥頭(切碎) ………1大匙
   椰子粉 ………………1杯

½ lb.(225g) fresh, tender string beans

1. 1 T. chopped onions
   1 t. salt
   1 red chili (split into two)
   ½ t. ea.(powder): cumin, turmeric

2. ½ t. ea.: mustard seeds, cumin seeds

   1 T. chopped shallot
   1 c. coconut flakes

1 菜豆摘去老筋，洗淨細切(圖1)，連同 1 料及水 ¾ 杯一起煮至汁收乾。

2 油2大匙燒熱，炒 2 料至爆裂後，加紅蔥頭略炒，再入菜豆及椰子粉拌炒1分鐘至均勻，趁熱與飯配食。

1 Remove the beantips and pull out the fibrous string from both sides. Wash and cut into thin crosswise slices (Fig.1). Add 1 to the beans and cook with ¾ c. water until dry.

2 Heat 2 T. oil and add 2. When they sputter add shallot and saute. Then add beans with coconut flakes and mix well. Stir for a minute. Serve hot with rice.

1

什錦蔬菜
Mixed Vegetable Stir-Fry

馬鈴薯、茄子、白花菜、
青椒、菠菜、莆瓜、南瓜
·············共12兩(450公克)

1　茴香子、芥茉子、小茴香子
　　·················各 ½ 小匙

　　洋蔥(切丁) ··········1大匙

2　薑泥、蒜泥 ········各1大匙
　　鬱金香粉 ············½ 小匙

3　紅糖(圖1) ···········1大匙
　　辣椒粉、鹽 ········各1小匙

　　肉桂粉 ···············1小匙

1 lb .(450g) mixed
  vegetables: potato,
  eggplant, cauliflower,
  green pepper, spinach,
  white gourd, pumpkin

1　½ t. ea.: fennel seeds,
   mustard seeds, cumin
   seeds

　 1 T. chopped onions

2　1 T. ea.(paste): garlic,
   ginger
   ½ t. turmeric powder

3　1 T. brown sugar (Fig.1)
   1 t. ea.: salt, chili powder

　 1 t. cinnamon powder

1　將所有蔬菜處理好並切成5公分長塊狀(圖2)。

2　油3大匙燒熱，先炒 1 料至爆裂，入洋蔥炒至微黃，再加 2 料炒香。續
　　入蔬菜及水 ¼ 杯拌勻，火轉小，加蓋煮約5分鐘，最後入 3 料拌炒至汁
　　收乾。

3　將肉桂粉撒在蔬菜上拌勻，趁熱食用。

□ 此為東印度地區普遍之菜餚。

1 Wash and chop all vegetables uniformly into 2" (5cm) long
  pieces (Fig. 2).

2 Heat 3 T. oil and add 1. When they sputter, add onions and stir
  until light brown. Add 2 and fry until fragrant. Then add
  vegetables with ¼ c. water and mix together. Lower heat and
  cook covered for 5 minutes. Add 3 and stir-fry the vegatables
  until completely dry.

3 Sprinkle cinnamon powder over the cooked vegetables. Stir well
  and serve hot.

□ A popular dish in East India.

1

2

蔬菜煎餅
Leafy Vegetable Cutlets

莧菜或菠菜(切碎) ……………
…………………6兩(225公克)
熟馬鈴薯泥 ……8兩(300公克)

[1] 洋蔥(切碎) ……………1杯
薑末 ……………1大匙

[2] 茴香粉、黑胡椒粉、鹽………
…………………各1小匙
小豆蔻粉 ……………½小匙

蛋(打散) ……………1個
麵包粉 ……………適量

½ lb.(225g) chopped
amaranthus or spinach
⅔ lb.(300g) boiled
mashed potatoes

[1] 1 c. chopped onions
1 T. chopped ginger

[2] 1 t. ea.: fennel powder,
black pepper powder,
salt
½ t. cardamom powder

1 beaten egg
bread crumbs for coating

1 油3大匙燒熱,炒香 [1] 料,入切碎之蔬菜炒約3分鐘至汁收乾,再入馬鈴薯泥及 [2] 料拌勻取出,並分製成14個直徑4公分之圓餅(圖1)。

2 油1杯燒熱,將圓餅先沾蛋液(圖2)再沾麵包粉(圖3),以中火炸2分鐘至兩面呈金黃色即成。可與米飯配食,或當點心沾番茄醬食用。

1 Heat 3 T. oil and fry [1] until fragrant. Add the chopped vegetable and cook for 3 minutes until dry. Add potatoes and [2], mix well and remove from heat. Shape to form 14 round cutlets 1 ¾" (4cm) in diameter (Fig. 1).

2 Dip each in beaten egg (Fig. 2) then in bread crumbs (Fig. 3). Set aside. Heat 1c. oil and fry the cutlets over medium heat for 2 minutes until both sides turn golden brown. Goes well with rice. The dish can also be served with tomato sauce as a snack item.

1

2

3

辣味白花菜

Spicy Cauliflower

白花菜(洗淨切小朵, 圖1)
　　　　……8兩(300公克)

小茴香子 ………………1小匙

1 ｜ 洋蔥泥(圖2) …………½ 杯
　　蒜泥、薑泥(圖2) …各 ½ 大匙

2 ｜ 胡荽粉 …………………1小匙
　　辣椒粉、鬱金香粉…各 ½ 小匙

3 ｜ 番茄(切丁) ……………1杯
　　鹽、糖 ……………各1小匙

香菜末 …………………½ 杯

⅔ lb. (300g) cauliflower
washed and cut into
small pieces (Fig.1)
1 t. cumin seeds

1 ｜ ½ c. ground onions (Fig.2)
　　½ T. ea. (paste): garlic,
　　ginger (Fig.2)

2 ｜ 1 t. coriander powder
　　½ t. ea. (powder): chili,
　　turmeric

3 ｜ 1 c. chopped tomatoes
　　1 t. ea: salt, sugar

½ c. chopped coriander
leaves

1 油3大匙燒熱，炒小茴香子至爆裂後，再加 1 料炒香。

2 火轉小，加 2 料拌炒均勻，再入 3 料續炒1分鐘至番茄混合均勻。

3 加入白花菜拌勻煮約5分鐘後，蓋鍋改小火再煮10分鐘至汁收乾，煮時略攪拌以免黏鍋。

4 撒上香菜後趁熱食用。

1 Heat 3 T. oil and add cumin seeds. When they sputter add 1 and saute until fragrant.

2 Lower heat, add 2 and stir. Add 3 and stir for a minute until the tomatoes are well blended.

3 Add the cauliflower and mix. Cook for about 5 minutes. Then cook covered for another 10 minutes over low heat until dry. Stir once or twice while cooking to prevent sticking.

4 Add coriander leaves, mix and serve hot.

1

2

椰香白花菜

Cauliflower and Coconut

白花菜(切碎或刨絲，圖1)
................8兩(300公克)

1 芥茉子、小茴香子 …各1小匙
　乾辣椒(切半) …………1個

2 洋蔥(切碎) …………1大匙
　鬱金香粉 …………1/2小匙

3 洋蔥(切碎) …………1大匙
　鹽 …………………1小匙
　小茴香粉 …………1/2小匙
　新鮮紅辣椒(直剖半) ……1條

椰子粉 ………………1杯

$^2/_3$ lb. (300g) shredded
cauliflower (Fig.1)

1 1 t. ea: mustard seeds,
　cumin seeds
　1 dry red chili cut into 2
　pieces

2 1 T. chopped onions
　1/2 t. turmeric powder

3 1 T. chopped onions
　1 t. salt
　1/2 t. cumin powder
　1 fresh red chili split into
　two

1 c. coconut flakes

1 油3大匙燒熱，炒 1 料至爆裂，再加 2 料炒至微黃。

2 加入花菜與 3 料拌炒均勻，再加水1/2杯，並將火轉小蓋鍋煮至熟軟且汁
收乾，煮時需攪拌使加熱均勻。

3 撒上椰子粉拌勻，熄火蓋鍋燜5分鐘即成，拌飯佳。

1 Heat 3 T. oil and add 1. When they sputter add 2 and fry until
slightly brown.

2 Add the cauliflower and 3, stir and add 1/2 c. water. Lower heat.
Cook covered until tender and dry. Stir occasionally to cook
evenly.

3 Add coconut flakes and mix well. Turn the heat off and keep
covered for 5 minutes before serving. Goes well with rice.

1

鑲青椒

Stuffed Green Pepper(Simla Mirch)

青椒 …………12兩(450公克)

① 洋蔥(切碎) ………………1杯
　 薑末 …………………………2大匙
　 紅辣椒末 …………………2小匙

② 胡荽粉………………………1½大匙
　 辣椒粉 ………………………½小匙
　 鬱金香粉 …………………¼小匙

③ 熟馬鈴薯泥 …12兩(450公克)
　 香菜末 ………………………½杯
　 鹽 ……………………………1小匙

1 lb.(450g) well shaped
　green peppers

① 1 c. chopped onions
　 2 T. chopped ginger
　 2 t. chopped red chilies

② 1½ T. coriander powder
　 ½ t. chili powder
　 ¼ t. turmeric powder

③ 1 lb.(450g) boiled mashed
　 potatoes
　 ½ c. chopped coriander
　 leaves
　 1 t. salt

1 青椒洗淨，小心在一邊劃一刀去籽(圖1)。

2 油2大匙燒熱炒香 ① 料，火轉小加 ② 料拌勻，再入 ③ 料混合成餡分別填
　入青椒內(圖2)。

3 油 ½ 杯燒熱，分批將青椒煎至顏色均勻變深，即成。

☐ 熟馬鈴薯泥亦可以熟絞肉取代。鑲好之青椒亦可置烤箱以375°F(190°C)
　每面烤20分鐘即成。

1 Wash and slit the green peppers on the side carefully, and
　remove the seeds (Fig.1).

2 Heat 2 T. oil and fry ① until fragrant. Lower heat, add ② and stir.
　Add ③ and combine all ingredients together. Divide the mixture
　into the same number of equal parts as the peppers. Carefully
　stuff each pepper with a portion (Fig. 2).

3 Heat about ½ c. oil; add 3-4 peppers at a time and shallow-fry
　until all sides are browned. Repeat the process with the
　remaining stuffed peppers.

☐ Potatoes can be substituted with cooked ground meat. The
　stuffed peppers can be baked in a preheated oven at 375°F
　(190°C) for 20 minutes on each side.

1

2

煎茄子

Fried Eggplant Slices

人份・Serves 4

茄子 ……………8兩(300公克)

1 | 鹽、黑胡椒粉、辣椒粉………
……………………各 ½ 小匙

2 | 檸檬汁 ………………1大匙

²⁄₃ lb. (300g) eggplant
(long variety)

1 | ½ t. ea.: salt, black pepper
powder, chili powder

2 | 1 T. lemon juice

1　茄子洗淨，切0.3公分厚斜片(圖1)，均勻撒上1小匙鹽並置30分鐘變軟後，略沖水拭乾(圖2)。

2　平底鍋燒熱，入油2大匙，待油熱後將茄子放入避免重疊，以中火每面煎1分鐘至兩面呈金黃色取出瀝乾油置盤，依法煎好所有茄子。

3　均勻撒上 1、2 料，趁熱食用。

1　Wash and cut the eggplant into oval shaped slices, ¹⁄₁₀" (**0.3cm**) thick (**Fig.1**).　Apply **1 t.** salt over the slices uniformly. Leave to sweat for half an hour.　Rinse and pat dry (**Fig.2**).

2　Heat a flat bottomed skillet and add **2 T.** oil. Arrange the slices on it without overlapping. Fry over medium heat for a minute on either side until golden brown.　Drain and arrange on a serving plate. Repeat the process with the remaining slices.

3　Sprinkle 1 and 2 uniformly over them, and serve hot.

1

2

32

咖哩馬鈴薯
Potato Ball Curry (Alu Dum)

馬鈴薯(約檸檬大) ‧‧‧‧‧‧‧‧‧‧‧‧‧‧
‧‧‧‧‧‧‧‧‧‧‧‧‧12兩(450公克)

[1] 洋蔥泥 ‧‧‧‧‧‧‧‧‧‧‧‧‧‧‧1/4 杯
蒜泥、薑泥 ‧‧‧‧‧‧‧‧各 1/2 大匙

[2] 胡荽粉、茴香粉 ‧‧‧‧‧‧各1小匙
肉桂粉、辣椒粉、小茴香粉
‧‧‧‧‧‧‧‧‧‧‧‧‧‧‧各 1/2 小匙
鬱金香粉 ‧‧‧‧‧‧‧‧‧‧‧‧1/4 小匙

[3] 番茄(切丁) ‧‧‧‧‧‧‧‧‧‧‧‧‧‧1杯
水 ‧‧‧‧‧‧‧‧‧‧‧‧‧‧‧‧‧‧3大匙
鹽 ‧‧‧‧‧‧‧‧‧‧‧‧‧‧‧‧‧‧1小匙

[4] 水 ‧‧‧‧‧‧‧‧‧‧‧‧‧‧‧‧‧1/2 杯
優格 ‧‧‧‧‧‧‧‧‧‧‧‧‧‧‧‧3大匙

香菜末 ‧‧‧‧‧‧‧‧‧‧‧‧‧‧‧1/2 杯

1 lb.(450g) small lemon
 sized potatoes

[1] 1/4 c. onion paste
 1/2 T. ea.(paste):garlic,
 ginger

[2] 1 t. ea. (powder):
 coriander, fennel
 1/2 t. ea.(powder):
 cinnamon, chili , cumin
 1/4 t. turmeric powder

[3] 1 c. chopped tomatoes
 3 T. water
 1 t. salt

[4] 1/2 c. water
 3 T. yogurt

 1/2 c. chopped coriander
 leaves

1 馬鈴薯洗淨，連皮煮至熟透後去皮備用。

2 油 1/2 杯燒熱，煎馬鈴薯至表面均勻呈金黃色取出。

3 用牙籤每隔2 1/2 公分於馬鈴薯表面刺洞(圖1)，使汁液易滲入。

4 餘油3大匙燒熱，炒香[1]料，火轉小，加[2]料拌炒後續入[3]料並蓋鍋煮1
 分鐘，將其拌成泥狀，再加[4]料拌勻，放入馬鈴薯蓋鍋再煮3-4分鐘至入
 味且汁收乾，撒上香菜即成。

1 Wash and boil potatoes with skin. Peel skin and set aside.

2 Heat 1/2 c. oil, fry the potatoes until golden brown all over and
 remove from oil.

3 Using a tooth pick, prick the potatoes 1" (2 1/2 cm) apart to allow
 the juices to penetrate (Fig.1).

4 Heat 3 T. of the remaining oil and saute [1] until fragrant. Lower
 heat, add [2] and fry. Add [3], mix and cook covered for a
 minute. Stir to make a paste. Add [4] and mix. Now add the fried
 potatoes. Simmer covered for **3-4** minutes so the potatoes may
 absorb the gravy. Add coriander leaves and serve.

1

莆瓜球

Bottle Gourd Balls (Vegetable Kofta)

[1] 莆瓜(去皮切絲，圖1)……2杯
洋蔥(切碎) ……………2大匙
紅辣椒末、薑末、蒜末………
…………………各1小匙
鹽 ………………………½小匙

[2] 酥炸粉(圖2)…………4大匙
麵粉 ……………………1大匙

調味汁:
洋蔥(切碎)……………½杯
[3] 蒜泥、薑泥 ………各½大匙

[4] 胡荽粉 …………………1大匙
茴香粉 …………………½小匙
辣椒粉、鬱金香粉…各¼小匙

[5] 番茄(切丁)、水 ……各½杯
鹽 ………………………½小匙

香菜末 …………………½杯

2 c. shredded bottle gourd,
(without the skin; Fig.1)

[1]
2 T. chopped onions
1 t. ea. (chopped): red
chili, ginger, garlic
½ t. salt

[2]
4 T. fryer mix powder (Fig. 2)
1 T. flour

For the sauce:
½ c. chopped onions

[3]
½ T. ea.(paste): garlic,
ginger

[4]
1 T. coriander powder
½ t. cumin powder
¼ t. ea. (powder): chili,
turmeric

[5]
½ c. ea.: chopped
tomatoes, water
½ t. salt

½ c. chopped coriander
leaves

1 將莆瓜絲之水份擠乾。加 [1] 料拌勻後，續入 [2] 料混合並做成16個球(圖3)。油1杯燒熱，炸莆瓜球至呈金黃色取出備用。

2 餘油2大匙炒洋蔥後，加 [3] 料炒香，火轉小，入 [4] 料略炒，再入 [5] 料並蓋鍋煮1分鐘，拌炒均勻後加水1½杯稀釋即為調味汁。

3 將炸好之莆瓜球放入調味汁中再煮5分鐘，最後撒上香菜裝飾即成。

1 Squeeze out the excess water from the shredded gourd, add [1] and mix. Then add [2], combine well, and make **16** balls (Fig. 3). Heat 1 c. oil, fry the balls until golden brown and set aside.

2 Use 2 T. of the remaining oil and saute the onions. Add [3] and fry until fragrant. Lower heat, add [4] and stir. Then add [5]. Cook covered for a minute. Mix until well blended. Then add 1½ c. water to dilute the sauce.

3 Drop in the fried balls and simmer for **5** minutes. Garnish with coriander leaves.

1

2

3

青豆馬鈴薯
Peas and Potatoes (Alu Mutter)

1 | 馬鈴薯(切1公分塊狀) ………
………6兩(225公克)
新鮮青豆仁…………1½ 杯

洋蔥(切碎) …………½ 杯

2 | 蒜泥、薑泥 ………各½ 大匙
茴香(略磨)、小茴香粉 ………
…………各1小匙

印度咖哩粉 …………1大匙

3 | 番茄(切丁) …………1杯
鹽 …………1小匙

4 | 香菜末 …………½ 杯
肉桂粉 …………½ 小匙

1 | ½ lb.(225g) potatoes, cut
in ½" (1cm) cubes
1 ½ c. fresh peas

½ c. chopped onions

2 | ½ T. ea.(paste): garlic,
ginger
1 t. ea.: coarsely ground
fennel, cumin powder

1 T. heaped Indian curry
powder

3 | 1 c. chopped tomato
1 t. salt

4 | ½ c. chopped coriander
leaves
½ t. cinnamon powder

1 油3大匙燒熱,加洋蔥炒至微黃,再入 2 料炒香。火轉小並入咖哩粉炒匀,再加 3 料拌炒1分鐘至均匀,最後加入 1 料及水1½ 杯,蓋鍋煮12分鐘至汁呈濃稠狀。

2 撒上 4 料稍攪拌,趁熱食用。

1 Heat 3 T. oil and fry the onions until almost brown. Add 2 and stir until fragrant. Lower heat, add the curry powder and stir well. Then add 3. Stir and cook for a minute until well blended. Add 1 with 1½ c. water and cook covered for 12 minutes until gravy thickens.

2 Sprinkle 4 on top; stir and serve hot.

35

青豆乾酪

Cottage Cheese and Peas (Paneer Mutter)

青豆 ⋯⋯⋯⋯⋯6兩(225公克)
自製乾酪* ⋯⋯⋯⋯⋯⋯⋯2杯
洋蔥(切碎) ⋯⋯⋯⋯⋯1杯
蒜泥、薑泥 ⋯⋯⋯⋯各1大匙

1 胡荽粉 ⋯⋯⋯⋯⋯⋯⋯1大匙
小茴香粉、辣椒粉、鬱金香粉
、黑胡椒粉 ⋯⋯各½小匙

2 番茄(切碎) ⋯⋯⋯⋯⋯1杯
鹽 ⋯⋯⋯⋯⋯⋯⋯⋯1½小匙

3 丁香粉、肉桂粉、小豆蔻粉、
茴香粉 ⋯⋯⋯⋯各½小匙

½ lb.(225g) peas
2 c. cottage cheese*
1 c. chopped onions
1 T. ea.: garlic paste, ginger
paste

1 1 T. coriander powder
½ t. ea. (powder): cumin,
chili, turmeric, black
pepper

2 1 c. chopped tomatoes
1½ t. salt

3 ½ t. ea. (powder): clove,
cinnamon, cardamom,
fennel

1 油3大匙燒熱，炒洋蔥至微黃，加蒜、薑泥炒香。

2 火轉小，入 1 料炒勻，加 2 料及水1杯，蓋鍋煮1分鐘後掀開拌勻。加青豆及水2杯，蓋鍋續煮5分鐘。

3 放入乾酪煮5分鐘，再撒上 3 料拌勻後趁熱食用。可以香菜末裝飾。

* 自製乾酪：

1 將奶粉2杯加水4杯沖泡成牛奶。

2 置鍋中加熱攪拌至開始沸騰，加檸檬汁3大匙且持續攪拌至牛奶沉澱(圖1)熄火備用。

3 以棉布包裹擠出水份(圖2)，並用重物平壓成一大片，1小時後取出即成乾酪(圖3)。切成1立方公分塊，約為2杯量。

1

2

3

1 Heat 3 T. oil and saute onions. When almost brown, add garlic-ginger paste and fry until fragrant.

2 Lower heat and add 1; stir to mix. Add 2 with 1 c. water. Cover and cook for a minute. Open the lid and mix well. Now add the peas with 2 c. water. Cover and cook for 5 minutes.

3 Add cheese and simmer for 5 minutes. Add 3, mix and serve hot. Garnish with chopped coriander leaves.

* Cottage cheese:

1 Add 4 c. water to 2 c. of any milk powder and mix well.

2 Heat in a hard bottom pan and bring to boil, then add 3 T. lemon juice and stir continuously until the water separates (Fig. 1). Remove from heat and set aside.

3 Strain and squeeze out the water using a piece of cloth (Fig. 2). Keep the cheese tight in the cloth and place a weight over this to flatten and set to a single piece. After an hour remove the cloth (Fig. 3) and cut into ½" (1cm) squares, making about 2 c.

煎魚

Fried Fish

鮮魚片(切1公分厚片，圖1)
　　………………8兩(300公克)

① 洋蔥泥 …………………1大匙
　 薑泥、鹽 …………………各1小匙
　 辣椒粉…………………1½小匙
　 胡椒粉 ………………¼小匙

⅔ lb. (300g) fish fillets, cut into ½" (1cm) thick pieces (Fig.1)

① 1 T. onion paste
　1 t. ea: ginger paste, salt
　1½ t. chili powder
　¼ t. pepper powder

1 魚片洗淨拭乾，放入調勻的①料內，醃2小時以上。

2 油1杯燒熱，一次放入2或3片魚以中火煎至兩面酥脆且呈金黃色即成。食時可撒上洋蔥圈及檸檬汁。

□ 若使用全魚則在魚兩面劃深刀(圖2)，醃時較易入味。

1 Wash fish fillets and pat dry. Mix ① thoroughly and apply evenly all over the fish. Marinate for at least 2 hours.

2 Heat 1 c. oil. Add 2 or 3 fish slices at a time and fry on medium heat until both sides are crisp and golden brown. Serve with onion rings and lemon wedges.

□ If a whole fish is used, make deep cuts on both sides (Fig. 2) to absorb the marinade.

1

2

醬燒鮮魚

Fried Fish Curry

鮮魚片 …………8兩(300公克)
芥茉子 ………………½小匙
洋蔥(切片) ……………1杯

1 | 薑末 ………………1大匙
　　蒜末 ………………1小匙

2 | 胡荽粉 ………………1大匙
　　辣椒粉 ………………½小匙
　　鬱金香粉 ……………¼小匙

3 | 水 …………………1杯
　　醋 …………………2大匙
　　鹽 …………………1小匙

椰奶* ………………………½杯

⅔ lb. (300g) fresh fish fillets
½ t. mustard seeds
1 c. sliced onions

1 | 1 T. chopped ginger
　　1 t. chopped garlic

2 | 1 T. coriander powder
　　½ t. chili powder
　　¼ t. turmeric powder

3 | 1 c. water
　　2 T. vinegar
　　1 t. salt

½ c. coconut milk*

1　參考煎魚做法(見37頁)將魚片煎至兩面微黃末酥脆前取出。

2　油3大匙燒熱，炒芥茉子至爆裂，隨入洋蔥炒至微黃，再加 1 料炒香。

3　火轉小，加 2 料炒勻，再入 3 料煮開1分鐘後，放入魚片續煮2-5分鐘。

4　倒入椰奶再煮1分鐘即成，趁熱與米飯配食。

＊　市面上有現成的椰奶出售，也可用椰奶粉2大匙加熱水½杯沖泡即可。

1　Fry the fish as in Fried Fish (see p. 37) but remove from oil before becoming crisp.

2　Heat 3 T. oil and add mustard seeds. When they sputter, add onions and fry until light brown. Add 1 and fry until fragrant.

3　Lower heat; add 2 and mix. Add 3 and boil for 1 minute. Add the fried fish and simmer for 2-5 minutes.

4　Add coconut milk over the fish; cook for 1 minute and serve hot with rice.

＊　Ready made cocount milk is available in the market. If coconut milk powder is used, prepare by adding 2 T. powder to ½ c. of hot water.

茄汁燒魚

Tomato Fish Curry

鮮魚片 …………8兩(300公克)

1️⃣ 鹽 ………………………1小匙
　 鬱金香粉 ………………½小匙

2️⃣ 洋蔥(切碎) ……………1大匙
　 蒜末 ……………………1小匙

3️⃣ 糖、鹽 ………………各1小匙
　 辣椒粉、肉桂粉 …各½小匙
　 小豆蔻(略敲) ……………2粒

4️⃣ 番茄(切丁)、水 ……各1杯

2/3 lb. (300g) fresh fish fillets

1️⃣ 1 t. salt
　 ½ t. turmeric powder

2️⃣ 1 T. chopped onions
　 1 t. chopped garlic

3️⃣ 1 t. ea.: sugar, salt
　 ½ t. ea.: chili powder,
　　　　　 cinnamon powder
　 2 crushed cardamoms

4️⃣ 1 c. ea.: chopped tomatoes,
　 water

1 魚片洗淨拭乾，1️⃣料調勻塗於魚片兩面，醃1小時以上。

2 平底鍋入油5大匙燒熱，放入魚片，每面煎2-3分鐘後取出備用。

3 油3大匙燒熱，炒香 2️⃣ 料至洋蔥微黃，加3️⃣料拌勻，續入4️⃣ 料以小火燒煮5分鐘。

4 將魚放入，以湯汁淋於魚片上，蓋鍋再煮5分鐘至湯汁濃稠即成，可淋於飯上食用。

☐ 此為東印度地區普遍之菜餚。

1 Wash fillets clean and pat dry. Mix 1️⃣ thoroughly and apply evenly on both sides of each piece; marinate for at least 1 hour.

2 Heat a flat bottomed skillet and add **5** T. oil. When the oil is hot fry the fish for **2-3** minutes on both sides. Remove and set aside.

3 Heat **3** T. oil and fry 2️⃣ until slightly brown. Add 3️⃣ and mix well; add 4️⃣ and simmer for **5** minutes over low heat.

4 Add the fried fish to this gravy, spoon some gravy over the fish, cover and cook for **5** more minutes until the gravy is thick. Remove and serve on a bed of rice.

☐ This dish is popular in East India.

椰香燒魚
Fish In Coconut

4人份 · Serves 4

沙丁魚或其它類似鮮魚(切2½
公分塊狀) …6兩(225公克)

<u>1</u> 楊桃或芒果切片(圖1)…1½ 杯

椰子粉 ………………………1½ 杯
紅蔥頭(切碎)、薑末 各1大匙
<u>2</u> 鹽 …………………………1½ 小匙
粗粒辣椒粉 ……………1小匙
鬱金香粉 ………………¼ 小匙

½ lb. (225g) sardines or any
similar variety, cut into 1"
(2½cm) pieces

<u>1</u> 1½ c. raw star fruit or raw
mango thinly sliced
(Fig.1)

1½ c. coconut flakes
1 T. ea.(chopped): shallot,
ginger
<u>2</u> 1 ½ t. salt
1 t. red chili flakes
¼ t. turmeric powder

1 魚洗淨。若使用芒果則先去皮。

2 將 <u>1</u>、<u>2</u> 料混合置鍋中並放入魚,加水蓋過魚片(圖2)燒煮至汁收乾後即成,煮時須翻拌使加熱均勻,與米飯配食佳。

☐ 此為南印度地區普遍之菜餚。

1 Clean and wash fish. If mango is used, remove skin.

2 In a cook pot combine <u>1</u> and <u>2</u> ; add fish. Pour water to cover the fish (Fig. 2) and cook covered until the water evaporates. Gently toss the cooking pot once or twice while cooking so that fish pieces are evenly done. Goes well with rice.

☐ This dish is popular in Southern India.

1

2

香辣燒魚

Coriander Fish Curry

魚片(切1公分薄片) ⋯⋯⋯⋯
⋯⋯⋯⋯⋯12兩(450公克)
芥茉子 ⋯⋯⋯⋯⋯½小匙

1　洋蔥(切片) ⋯⋯⋯⋯⋯1杯
　　薑絲 ⋯⋯⋯⋯⋯⋯⋯1大匙
　　蒜(切片)、紅辣椒末　各1小匙

椰子粉 ⋯⋯⋯⋯⋯⋯3大匙

2　胡荽粉 ⋯⋯⋯⋯⋯⋯3大匙
　　辣椒粉、胡椒粉、鬱金香粉⋯
　　⋯⋯⋯⋯⋯⋯⋯各½小匙

3　水 ⋯⋯⋯⋯⋯⋯⋯1½杯
　　醋 ⋯⋯⋯⋯⋯⋯⋯1大匙
　　鹽 ⋯⋯⋯⋯⋯⋯⋯1小匙

椰奶(見38頁)⋯⋯⋯⋯½杯

1 lb.(450g) fish, cut into
　½" (1cm) thin slices
½ t. mustard seeds

1　1 c. sliced onions
　　1 T. thin ginger strips
　　1 t. ea.: garlic slices,
　　　chopped red chilies

3 T. coconut flakes

2　3 T. coriander powder
　　½ t. ea. (powder): chili,
　　　pepper, turmeric

3　1½ c. water
　　1 T. vinegar
　　1 t. salt

½ c. coconut milk (see p.
38)

1　油2大匙燒熱，炒芥茉子至爆裂，並入①料炒至微黃。

2　火轉小，加椰子粉攪拌煮1分鐘，隨入②料拌勻，再加③料煮開後，放入魚片續煮7-10分鐘至汁濃稠。

3　淋上椰奶再煮1分鐘即成，以香菜裝飾，且可與米飯配食。

1　Heat 2 T. oil and add mustard seeds. When they sputter, add ① and stir until light brown.

2　Lower heat; add coconut flakes, stir and cook for a minute. Add ② and mix well. Add ③ and boil. Add fish and cook 7-10 minutes until the gravy thickens.

3　Add coconut milk and simmer for a minute; remove from heat. Garnish with coriander leaves and serve with rice.

茄汁蝦皮

Dry Shrimp Flakes In Tomato Gravy

乾蝦皮(圖1) ·····················1杯

[1] 洋蔥(切碎) ·················1杯
　　薑末、蒜末 ···········各1大匙

[2] 辣椒粉 ·······················1小匙
　　鬱金香粉 ···············¼小匙

[3] 番茄(切丁) ···············1½杯
　　水 ·····························½杯
　　鹽 ·····························¾小匙

1 c. dry shrimp flakes (Fig.1)

[1] 1 c. chopped onions
　　1 T. ea. (chopped): ginger, garlic

[2] 1 t. chili powder
　　¼ t. turmeric powder

[3] 1½ c. chopped tomatoes
　　½ c. water
　　¾ t. salt

1 油1杯燒熱，入蝦皮炸1分鐘撈出(圖2)瀝乾備用。

2 餘油4大匙炒香 [1] 料，火轉小，入 [2] 料拌炒，加 [3] 料燒煮1分鐘至番茄丁混合均勻。

3 放入煎好的蝦皮及水1杯燒煮2分鐘即成，與米飯配食佳。

1 Heat 1 c. oil and deep fry shrimp flakes for 1 minute. Drain (Fig. 2) and set aside.

2 Fry [1] in 4 T remaining oil until fragrant. Lower heat; add [2] and stir to mix well. Add [3] and cook for 1 minute until tomatoes are well blended.

3 Add the fried shrimp flakes with 1 c. water and cook for 2 minutes. Serve with rice.

1

2

蝦皮莆瓜

Dry Shrimp Flakes with Gourd

乾蝦皮 ·················· ½ 杯
莆瓜(切1公分塊狀) ···········
··············6兩(225公克)

① 椰子粉 ·················· ½ 杯
洋蔥(切碎) ·············1大匙
辣椒粉、薑末 ········各1小匙
鹽 ···················· ½ 小匙
腰果 ············6粒(無亦可)

芥茉子 ·················· ½ 小匙
紅蔥頭(切碎) ·············1粒

½ c. dry shrimp flakes
½ lb.(225g) gourd, cut into
    ½" (1cm) cubes

① ½ c. coconut flakes
1 T. chopped onions
1 t.ea.: chili powder,
    chopped ginger
½ t. salt
6 cashew nuts (optional)

½ t. mustard seeds
1 chopped shallot

1 將乾蝦皮、莆瓜、① 料加水1½ 杯蓋鍋煮5分鐘備用。

2 油2大匙燒熱,炒芥茉子至爆裂,再入紅蔥頭拌炒至微黃取出,淋於煮好之蝦皮莆瓜上拌勻,與米飯配食。

1 Cook the shrimp, gourd and ① in 1½ c. water covered for 5 minutes.

2 Heat 2 T. oil and add mustard seeds. When they sputter, add the shallot and fry until brown. Pour over the cooked dish. Mix and serve with rice.

煎魚餅

Fish Cutlets

1 | 洋蔥(切碎) ················· 1/2 杯
| 薑末 ····················· 1大匙
| 紅辣椒(去籽、切碎) ···1小匙

胡椒粉 ··················· 1/2 小匙
麵包粉 ··················· 3/4 杯

2 | 熟魚肉(去骨、壓碎，圖1)* ···
| ······················· 2杯
| 鹽 ······················ 1小匙

蛋(打散) ··············· 1個

1 | 1/2 c. chopped onions
| 1 T. chopped ginger
| 1 t. chopped red chili
| without seeds

1/2 t. pepper powder
3/4 c. bread crumbs

2 | 2 c. fish (boned, boiled and
| shredded; Fig.1)*
| 1 t. salt

1 beaten egg

1 油2大匙燒熱，炒香 ① 料取出，拌入胡椒粉及麵包粉，並撒水2-3大匙，混勻放置1分鐘使麵包粉軟化較易沾粘。

2 加入 ② 料拌勻，並做成12個直徑5公分之魚餅(圖2)備用。

3 油 3/4 杯燒熱，將魚餅沾蛋液後，放入油中煎至兩面呈金黃色即成。隨時調整火候以防燒焦，趁熱淋上檸檬汁與洋蔥片配食。

＊ 鮮魚片約12兩(450公克)加水1杯煮至收乾且肉熟後壓碎。

1 Heat 2 T. oil and saute ① until fragrant; remove and add pepper powder and bread crumbs. Sprinkle 2-3 T. water, mix well and wait for 1 minute for bread crumbs to become soft.

2 Add ② and mix. Make 12 small cutlets, 2" (5cm) in diameter (Fig. 2). Set aside.

3 Heat 3/4 c. oil until smoking hot, dip each cutlet in beaten egg and carefully fry them until both sides are golden brown. Adjust heat to avoid burning the cutlets. Serve hot with lemon and onion slices.

＊ Cook about 1 lb. (450g) of fish fillets in 1 c. water until dry. Shred them when cooked.

1

2

香烤鯧魚
Baked Pomfret

鯧魚1條 ………8兩(300公克)

① 辣椒粉 ……………………1小匙
胡椒粉、鬱金香粉 各 1/2 小匙

② 洋蔥泥 ……………………1大匙
蒜泥、薑泥 ………各 1/2 大匙
鹽 ……………………1/2 小匙

2/3 lb. (300g) pomfret

① 1 t. chili powder
1/2 t. ea: pepper powder,
   turmeric powder

② 1 T. onion paste
1/2 T. ea.: garlic paste,
   ginger paste
1/2 t. salt

1 鯧魚去除內臟、鰭及尾並洗淨，魚身兩面劃深刀。乾鍋炒 ① 料1分鐘後取出備用。

2 ①、② 料拌勻塗於魚身內外及劃刀處，醃2小時。

3 將魚包上鋁箔紙，用叉子刺洞(圖1)，置預熱烤箱以350°F(180°C)烤30分鐘至熟，趁熱淋上檸檬汁食用。

1 Prepare fish by removing the entrails, gills, fins and tail. Wash thoroughly and make deep cuts on both sides of the fish (see p. 37). In a dry skillet roast ① for a minute and set aside.

2 Mix ① and ② well to form a smooth paste. Apply over fish evenly inside the stomach and also in the gashes. Marinate for about 2 hours.

3 Wrap fish completely in a baking foil and perforate with a fork (Fig. 1). Bake in a preheated oven at 350°F (180°C) for 30 minutes or until done. Serve hot with lemon wedges.

1

檸檬香魚

Fish In Lemon

鮮魚片(去皮) …8兩(300公克)

鮮魚片(去皮) …8兩(300公克)

① 紅蔥頭(每粒縱切半,圖1) 2杯
檸檬汁 ……………………2大匙
紅辣椒(約5公分,剖半) …1條
鹽 ……………………………1小匙
鬱金香粉 …………………¼小匙

胡椒粉……………………少許

⅔ lb. (300g) fish fillets
   (skinned)

2 c. shallots (each cut
   lengthwise in 2, Fig.1)
① 2 T. lemon juice
1 red chili (split), 2" (5cm) in
   length
1 t. salt
¼ t. turmeric powder

a pinch of pepper powder
   for garnish

1 將魚片、① 料及水1杯以中火蓋鍋煮5分鐘至汁完全收乾。

2 分別將魚片及紅蔥頭撈出排盤,再撒上胡椒粉趁熱食用。

1 Mix fish and ① with 1 c. water and cook covered for 5 minutes over medium heat until the water evaporates.

2 Place fillets on a serving plate and serve with cooked shallots. Sprinkle pepper on top and serve hot.

1

辣味鯖魚
Mackerel In Chili Sauce

鯖魚(切2½公分厚塊) ⋯⋯⋯⋯
⋯⋯⋯⋯⋯⋯8兩(300公克)
芥茉子 ⋯⋯⋯⋯⋯½小匙

1
洋蔥(切丁) ⋯⋯⋯⋯⋯½ 杯
薑末 ⋯⋯⋯⋯⋯1小匙
紅辣椒末 ⋯⋯⋯⋯⋯½ 小匙

2
辣椒粉、胡荽粉 ⋯⋯各1大匙
鬱金香粉 ⋯⋯⋯⋯¼ 小匙

3
醋 ⋯⋯⋯⋯⋯⋯⋯⋯1大匙
鹽 ⋯⋯⋯⋯⋯⋯⋯⋯1小匙

⅔ lb.(300g) mackerel cut
   into 1" (2 ½ cm) thick
   pieces
½ t. mustard seeds

1
½ c. chopped onions
1 t. chopped ginger
½ t. chopped red chili

2
1 T. ea.: chili powder,
   coriander powder
¼ t. turmeric powder

3
1 T. vinegar
1 t. salt

1 魚片洗淨備用。

2 油4大匙燒熱，炒芥茉子至爆裂，入 ① 料炒1分鐘。火轉小，加 ② 料拌炒均勻，再入 ③ 料、水1杯及魚片，蓋鍋燒煮10分鐘即成，其濃湯汁拌飯佳。

1 Wash and clean fish. Set aside.

2 Heat **4** T. oil and add mustard seeds. When they sputter, add ①
and saute for a minute. Lower heat, add ② and mix well. Add ③,
1 c. water and the fish. Cook covered for **10** minutes. The thick
gravy goes well with rice.

茄汁煎魚

Fried Fish in Tomato Juice

沙丁魚或其它魚(切5公分長
　塊) ‥‥‥‥‥8兩(300公克)
番茄‥‥‥‥‥‥6兩(225公克)

1 ⎡ 辣椒粉 ‥‥‥‥‥‥‥‥1小匙
　⎢ 鹽 ‥‥‥‥‥‥‥‥‥‥½小匙
　⎣ 胡椒粉 ‥‥‥‥‥‥‥‥¼小匙

2 ⎡ 洋蔥(切片) ‥‥‥‥‥‥1杯
　⎢ 薑末 ‥‥‥‥‥‥‥‥‥1小匙
　⎣ 蒜(略拍) ‥‥‥‥‥‥‥2瓣

3 ⎡ 辣椒粉 ‥‥‥‥‥‥‥‥1小匙
　⎣ 鹽 ‥‥‥‥‥‥‥‥‥‥½小匙

⅔ lb.(300g) sardines or any
　fish cut into 2" (5cm) long
　pieces
½ lb. (225g) tomatoes

1 ⎡ 1 t. chili powder
　⎢ ½ t. salt
　⎣ ¼ t. pepper powder

2 ⎡ 1 c. sliced onions
　⎢ 1 t. chopped ginger
　⎣ 2 cloves of garlic
　　(crushed)

3 ⎡ 1 t. chili powder
　⎣ ½ t. salt

1 魚片洗淨。①料調勻塗於魚片上，醃1小時。

2 番茄切2或3大塊，加水2杯煮開，待冷榨汁並濾除殘渣(圖1)。

3 油½杯燒熱，將魚煎至兩面呈金黃色且熟透取出備用。

4 餘油2大匙燒熱，炒②料至洋蔥微黃。火轉小，隨入③料炒勻，並加番茄汁燒開，再入魚片蓋鍋煮5-6分鐘至湯汁濃稠即成，與米飯配食佳。

1 Wash and clean the fish. Mix ① thoroughly and apply evenly on fish. Marinate for 1 hour.

2 Cut the tomatoes into 2 or 3 large pieces and boil in 2 c. water. Squeeze out the juice and strain (Fig.1) when it cools to room temperature.

3 Heat ½ c. oil and fry fish until both sides are brown and done. Remove and set aside.

4 Heat 2 T. of the remaining oil and saute ② until onions turn slightly brown. Lower heat; add ③ and stir. Add the prepared tomato juice and bring to boil. Add the fried fish and cook covered for **5** to **6** minutes until the gravy becomes thick. Goes well with rice.

1

辣味大蝦

Fried Spicy Prawns

大蝦(燙熟去殼、去腸泥) ……
……………6兩(225公克)

1 | 原味優格 ………………1杯
蒜泥、薑泥、檸檬汁或醋……
………………各1大匙
辣椒粉 ………………1小匙
鹽 ………………½小匙
胡椒粉、鬱金香粉…各¼小匙

紅色食用色素 …少許(無亦可)

½ lb.(225g) boiled prawns
shelled and deveined

1 | 1 c. plain yogurt
1 T. ea.: garlic paste, ginger
paste, lemon juice or
vinegar
1 t. chili powder
½ t. salt
¼ t. ea.: pepper powder,
turmeric powder

A few drops of red edible
color (optional)

1 油2大匙燒熱,加 1 料以中火邊煮邊攪拌至汁濃稠,入大蝦及色素燒煮
至辣汁均勻沾於蝦上,取出置盤或與醬汁淋於飯上食用。

1 Heat **2** T. oil and fry 1 over medium heat. Stir continuously until
the gravy becomes thick. Add prawns and color. Stir until they
are well coated. Remove the prawns from the gravy and
arrange on a plate or serve them over rice with the gravy.

魚肉蛋餅
Fish Omelet

熟魚肉(去骨、壓碎, 見44頁)
....................................1杯

1️⃣
洋蔥(切碎) ....½杯
椰子粉 2大匙
紅辣椒末、薑末 各1小匙
鹽、醋 ....各½小匙
胡椒粉、鬱金香粉 各¼小匙

蛋(打散) 3個

1 c. cooked fish flakes
   (shredded without bones;
   see p. 44)

1️⃣
½ c. chopped onions
2 T. coconut flakes
1 t. ea. (chopped): red chili,
   ginger
½ t. ea.: salt, vinegar
¼ t. ea.: pepper powder,
   turmeric powder

3 beaten eggs

1 將熟魚肉與 1️⃣ 料拌勻，再加入蛋液攪拌均勻。

2 平底鍋燒熱，塗上1大匙油，並倒入 ¼ 份的魚肉混合物，煎成薄餅狀(圖1)，待兩面均熟後即成，同法煎其餘3蛋餅，並趁熱食用。

1 Mix the fish flakes and 1️⃣ together. Then add the beaten eggs and mix.

2 Heat a flat skillet, smear 1 T. oil, pour out ¼ portion of the mixture and spread evenly to form a pancake (Fig. 1). Cook on both sides until done. Prepare 3 more pancakes, similarly. Serve hot.

1

香燒魚

Fish in White Sauce

鮮魚片(去皮、切大塊) ………
……………8兩(300公克)
熟青豆仁、熟紅蘿蔔粗絲* …
…………各½杯(50公克)
奶油 …………………1大匙
麵粉 …………………1大匙
椰奶 …………………¾ 杯
胡椒粉 ………………¾ 小匙

1 | 小茴香子、芥茉子、丁香粒…
 | ………………各½ 小匙
 | 肉桂片 ………………½公分

2 | 洋蔥(切絲)……………½ 杯
 | 薑末 …………………1大匙
 | 紅辣椒末、蒜末 ……各1小匙

3 | 醋 ……………………1大匙
 | 鹽 ……………………1小匙

⅔ lb.(300g) fish fillets
 (skinned and cut in
 chunks)

½ c. ea. (cooked): peas,
 chopped carrots*
1 T. butter
1 T. flour
¾ c. coconut milk
¾ t. pepper powder

1 | ½ t. ea.: cumin seeds,
 | mustard seeds, cloves
 | ½ " (1 cm). cinnamon piece

2 | ½ c. sliced onions
 | 1 T. chopped ginger
 | 1 t. ea. (chopped): red chili,
 | garlic

3 | 1 T. vinegar
 | 1 t. salt

1 奶油於平底鍋加熱融化，加入麵粉炒勻後，緩緩加入椰奶(圖1)並邊攪拌以防結塊，持續加熱使呈濃稠，撒入胡椒粉即成白色拌料(圖2)。

2 油4大匙燒熱，炒 1 料至爆裂，入 2 料炒香後倒入白色拌料內。

3 鮮魚加 3 料及水1杯煮約10分鐘，再加入白色拌料拌勻，並以青豆仁、紅蘿蔔裝飾即成。

* 生青豆仁及紅蘿蔔粗絲可以水 ½ 杯加鹽 ⅛ 小匙煮熟。可選用任何可增加菜色變化之蔬菜。

1 Heat butter in a skillet. As it melts, add flour; stir and roast without loosing its color. Add milk gradually (Fig. 1) stirring to prevent the formation of lumps. Heat and thicken the sauce; add pepper, stir and set aside (Fig. 2).

2 Heat 4 T. oil and add 1. When they sputter, add 2 and saute until fragrant, then add to the sauce.

3 Cook fish with 3 and 1 c. water for about 10 minutes, then add to the prepared sauce. Mix well and serve with vegetables.

* Boil raw peas and carrots in ½ c. water with ⅛ t. salt until done. Any vegetable that could add color to this dish may be used

1

2

印度咖哩雞㈠

4人份 · Serves 4

Indian Chicken Curry I

雞塊(去皮) ……8兩(300公克)
馬鈴薯塊 ………4兩(150公克)
洋蔥(切片) ………………2杯

☐1 丁香、豆蔻(圖1,略磨) 各3粒
   茴香子(圖1,略磨) ……2小匙

蒜泥、薑泥 …………各1大匙

☐2 胡荽粉 ……………………1½ 大匙
   小茴香粉 …………………1小匙
   辣椒粉、胡椒粉、鬱金香粉
   …………………………各 ½ 小匙

☐3 醋 ………………………1大匙
   鹽 ………………………1小匙

椰奶(見38頁)……………½ 杯
肉桂粉 ……………………½ 小匙

⅔ lb. (300g) skinless chicken pieces
⅓ lb. (150g) potato pieces
2 c. sliced onions

☐1 3 ea. (ground coarsely): cloves, cardamoms (Fig.1)
   2 t. coarsely ground fennel seeds (Fig.1)

1 T. ea.: garlic paste, ginger paste

☐2 1 ½ T. coriander powder
   1 t. cumin powder
   ½ t. ea.(powder): chili, pepper, turmeric

☐3 1 T. vinegar
   1 t. salt

½ c. coconut milk (see p. 38)
½ t. cinnamon powder

1 油½杯燒熱,入洋蔥1杯炒至微黃,取出備用。

2 餘油炒另1杯之洋蔥至變色,加 ☐1 料拌勻,續入蒜、薑泥炒香。

3 火轉小,再入 ☐2 料炒拌後,隨入 ☐3 料、馬鈴薯塊及雞塊煮約1分鐘,加水2杯蓋鍋續煮15分鐘,煮時須攪拌1-2次。

4 倒入椰奶拌勻,蓋鍋再煮3-4分鐘至肉熟軟,加肉桂粉拌勻,並撒上炒好之洋蔥即成。

☐ 此為南印度地區普遍之菜餚。

1 Heat ½ c. oil and fry 1 c. onions until light brown; remove and set aside.

2 In remaining oil saute the next cup of onions until color changes. Add ☐1 and mix well. Add garlic paste, ginger paste and fry until fragrant.

3 Lower heat; add ☐2 and stir. Add ☐3, potatoes and chicken pieces and saute for a minute. Add 2 c. water and cook covered for 15 minutes. Stir once or twice when cooking.

4 Add coconut milk; stir and simmer covered for another 3-4 minutes until done. Add cinnamon powder and mix well. Sprinkle the fried onions on top and serve.

☐ This dish is popular in Southern India.

1

印度咖哩雞㈡

Indian Chicken Curry II

雞塊(去皮) …12兩(450公克)

① 優格 ……………………2大匙
　 鹽 ………………………1½小匙

② 洋蔥末、香菜末 ………各2杯
　 薑末 ……………………2大匙
　 蒜末 ……………………1大匙
　 水 ………………………½杯

③ 胡荽粉 …………………1大匙
　 辣椒粉、小茴香粉、茴香粉…
　 　……………………各1小匙
　 鬱金香粉 ………………½小匙

④ 肉桂片(圖1) ………2½公分
　 豆蔻(略敲,圖1)…………2個
　 丁香、胡椒粒(圖1)……各4粒

番茄(切丁) ………………1杯

1 lb.(450g) skinless chicken
　pieces

① 2 T. yogurt
　 1½ t. salt

② 2 c. ea. (chopped): onions,
　　coriander leaves
　 2 T. chopped ginger
　 1 T. chopped garlic
　 ½ c. water

③ 1 T. coriander powder
　 1 t. ea. (powder): chili,
　　cumin, fennel
　 ½ t. turmeric powder

④ 1" (2½ cm)piece cinnamon
　　(Fig.1)
　 2 crushed cardamoms
　　(Fig.1)
　 4 ea.: cloves, pepper corns
　　(Fig.1)

1 c. chopped tomatoes

1 將雞塊放入 ① 料醃2小時(圖2)。

2 ② 料置於攪拌機中攪成泥,入 ③ 料拌勻成佐料備用。

3 油3大匙燒熱後入 ④ 料,當鍋中啪啪作響時加入調好的佐料,拌炒至香
　味溢出。

4 隨入番茄略炒,再入雞塊及醃汁拌勻後,加水2½杯蓋鍋以中火煮約20
　分鐘至肉熟軟,煮時須攪拌1-2次。可拌飯或與任何麥麵包配食。

□ 此為北印度地區普遍之菜餚。

1 Marinate the chicken in ① for 2 hours (Fig.2).

2 In a blender, grind ② into a paste.　Add ③ to this and mix, set
　aside.

3 Heat 3 T. oil and add ④; when it sputters, add the spice paste
　and stir until the aroma is released.

4 Add the tomatoes and mix. Now add the marinated chicken
　with the juice, stir. Then add 2½ c. water; cook covered over
　medium heat for about 20 minutes until done.　Stir once or twice
　while cooking. Goes very well with rice or any wheat bread.

□ This dish is popular in Northern India.

1

2

辣味炒雞塊
Spicy Fried Chicken

雞塊(去皮) …12兩(450公克)

[1]
胡荽粉 …………………3大匙
辣椒粉、丁香粉、鹽、醋……
……………………各1小匙
胡椒粉、小茴香粉、鬱金香粉
、肉桂粉 ………各 ½ 小匙

洋蔥(切薄片) ……………1杯

1 lb. (450g) skinless chicken
  pieces

[1]
3 T. coriander powder
1 t. ea.: chili powder, clove
   powder, salt, vinegar
½ t. ea. (powder): pepper,
   cumin, turmeric,
   cinnamon

1 c. onion slices

1　將雞塊加 [1] 料及水2杯煮20分鐘至肉熟軟。

2　油½杯燒熱，炒洋蔥至微黃，加入煮好的雞塊，以小火翻拌煮至汁收乾即成。

1　Cook chicken with [1] and **2** c. water for **20** minutes until done.

2　Heat ½ c. oil and fry the onions until they change color slightly. Add the cooked meat. Stir and saute on low heat until roasted dry.

香燜雞

Stewed Chicken

雞塊(去皮) …12兩(450公克)

① 洋蔥(切片) ……………………1杯
薑絲、紅辣椒末 ……各1大匙
小豆蔻、丁香(均略敲) 各3粒
肉桂片…………………約2 1/2 公分
茴香子(略磨) ………1 1/2 小匙

② 胡荽粉 ………………………1大匙
胡椒粉 …………………1/2 小匙

③ 水 …………………………………2杯
鹽 …………………………………1小匙

④ 麵粉 ………………………………1大匙
水 ………………………………1/4 杯

椰奶(見38頁) ……………1杯

1 lb.(450g) skinless chicken
   pieces

1 c. sliced onions
1 T. ea.: sliced ginger,
   chopped red chili
① 3 ea. (crushed):
   cardamoms, cloves
   1" (2 1/2cm) piece cinnamon
   1 1/2 t. coarsely ground fennel
   seeds

② 1 T. coriander powder
   1/2 t. pepper powder

③ 2 c. water
   1 t. salt

④ 1 T. flour
   1/4 c. water

1 c. coconut milk (see p. 38)

1 油3大匙燒熱,炒香 ① 料,續入 ② 料炒勻,再加 ③ 料及雞塊以中火蓋鍋
  煮15分鐘。

2 入調勻的 ④ 料續煮3-4分鐘至雞肉熟軟,倒入椰奶並煮至汁變濃稠即成,
  可與各式麥麵包一起食用。

1 Heat 3 T.oil and fry ① until fragrant. Add ② and stir to mix, add ③
  and the chicken. Cook covered for **15** minutes over medium
  heat.

2 Mix ④ and add to the chicken. Cook for **3-4** minutes until   well
  done. Then add the coconut milk and simmer for a few minutes
  until the gravy is thick. Goes well with any wheat bread.

烤雞肉串

Barbecued Chicken (Chicken Kababs)

雞肉塊(去皮，圖1) ············
··················8兩(300公克)

①
優格 ···················1/2 杯
香菜末 ···············2大匙
蒜泥、薑泥、洋蔥泥 各1大匙
辣椒粉 ················1小匙
胡椒粉、小茴香粉、鹽········
·······················各 1/2 小匙
鬱金香粉 ···········1/4 小匙

長的金屬串肉針··········適量

2/3 lb.(300g) chicken pieces
(boneless and skinless;
Fig.1)

①
1/2 c. yogurt
2 T. chopped coriander
leaves
1 T. ea.: garlic paste, ginger
paste, onion paste
1 t. chili powder
1/2 t. ea.: pepper powder,
cumin powder, salt
1/4 t. turmeric powder

long metal skewers

1 將 ① 料調勻成醬汁，入雞塊拌醃並冷藏12小時。

2 將雞塊串在串肉針上，直接在火上或烤肉架上烤熟(烤時略轉動)，可置於飯上或沾辣醬食用。

□ 可以番茄塊、青椒、洋蔥等和雞肉串成一串，來變化口味並增色。

1 Mix ① to form a smooth paste. Cover each piece of chicken with the paste and refrigerate for 12 hours.

2 String them on metal skewers and cook directly over a fire or on grill bars. Turn several times while cooking. Serve hot on a bed of rice or with any hot sauce.

□ Small tomato pieces, green peppers, onions etc. can also be strung along the meat for variation and color.

1

蔬菜炒雞塊
Chicken and Vegetables

雞肉塊(去皮) …8兩(300公克)
豌豆、紅蘿蔔、四季豆、
　　白花菜 ……共6兩(225公克)

1
水 ……………………½ 杯
奶油 ……………………½ 大匙
鹽 ……………………½ 小匙
胡椒粉 ………………¼ 小匙

2
胡荽粉 …………………1小匙
辣椒粉 …………………½ 小匙
鬱金香粉 ……………¼ 小匙

3
洋蔥(切丁)、油 ……各2大匙
薑末 ……………………1大匙
紅辣椒末、鹽 ………各1小匙
胡椒粉 ………………¼ 小匙
番茄(切丁)………………¾ 杯
優格 ……………………¼ 杯

⅔ lb.(300g) skinless chicken
　pieces
½ lb.(225g) mixed
　vegetables: peas, carrots,
　french beans, cauliflower

1
½ c. water
½ T. butter
½ t. salt
¼ t. pepper powder

2
1 t. coriander powder
½ t. chili powder
¼ t. turmeric powder

3
2 T. ea.: chopped onions, oil
1 T. chopped ginger
1 t. ea.: chopped red chili,
　salt
¼ t. pepper powder
¾ c. chopped tomatoes
¼ c. yogurt

1 紅蘿蔔及四季豆洗淨切成 2 ½ 公分長，白花菜切小朵。

2 將全部蔬菜加 ① 料煮至水收乾備用。

3 鍋燒熱略烤 ② 料(圖1)約半分鐘，入 ③ 料、雞塊及水1杯混勻，蓋鍋以中
　火煮20分鐘至水收乾。

4 打開蓋子將雞塊翻拌均勻，盛盤並以煮好之蔬菜裝飾，趁熱食用。

1 Wash and chop the carrot and beans into 1"(2 ½ cm) pieces.
　Cut the cauliflower into small florets.

2 Cook the vegetables with ① until the water is absorbed.

3 Heat a wok and lightly roast ② for half a minute (Fig.1). Add ③
　and chicken pieces; add 1 c. water mix well and cook covered
　over medium heat for 20 minutes until the water is absorbed.

4 Remove the lid and roast the chicken until the pieces are well
　coated. Arrange in a serving plate and garnish with the cooked
　vegetables. Serve hot.

1

檸汁雞塊

Tangy Chicken Curry

雞塊(去皮) …12兩(450公克)

[1] 薑泥、蒜泥 …………各1大匙

[2]
胡荽粉 ………………1大匙
小茴香粉 ……………1小匙
辣椒粉、胡椒粉 …各 1/2 小匙
鬱金香粉 ……………1/4 小匙

[3]
優格 …………………2大匙
檸檬汁 ………………1大匙
醬油 …………………1小匙
鹽 …………………… 3/4 小匙

香菜末 ………………1/2 杯

1 lb.(450g) skinless chicken
pieces

[1] 1 T. ea.: ginger paste, garlic
paste

[2]
1 T. coriander powder
1 t. cumin powder
1/2 t. ea. (powder): chili,
pepper
1/4 t. turmeric powder

[3]
2 T. yogurt
1 T. lemon juice
1 t. soy sauce
3/4 t. salt

1/2 c. chopped coriander
leaves

1 平底鍋入油 1/2 杯燒熱,將雞塊放入煎至兩面微黃取出備用。

2 餘油炒香 [1] 料,入 [2] 料炒勻,再加 [3] 料、雞塊及水2杯,以小火蓋鍋煮20分鐘至肉熟軟,撒上香菜末,並趁熱鋪在飯上食用。

1 Heat 1/2 c. oil in a flat skillet and fry chicken pieces until both sides are slightly brown. Remove and set aside.

2 In remaining oil fry [1] until fragrant. Add [2] and mix well. Then add [3], chicken and 2 c. water; cook covered for **20** minutes over low heat until the meat is tender. Garnish with chopped coriander leaves and serve over a bed of rice.

薯片煎肉

Roasted Meat with Potato Garnish

肉塊 ⋯⋯⋯⋯⋯8兩(300公克)
馬鈴薯 ⋯⋯⋯⋯4兩(150公克)

① 胡荽粉、醋 ⋯⋯⋯各1大匙
辣椒粉、鹽 ⋯⋯⋯各½小匙
鬱金香粉 ⋯⋯⋯⋯¼小匙
水 ⋯⋯⋯⋯⋯⋯⋯1杯

洋蔥(切片) ⋯⋯⋯⋯1杯

② 蒜(略拍，圖1) ⋯⋯⋯1大匙
胡椒粒(略拍，圖1) ⋯⋯1小匙

⅔ lb.(300g) meat pieces
   (any kind)
⅓ lb.(150g) potatoes

① 1 T. ea.: coriander powder,
      vinegar
   ½ t. ea.: chili powder, salt
   ¼ t. turmeric powder
   1 c. water

1 c. sliced onions

② 1 T. crushed garlic (Fig.1)
   1 t. crushed pepper corns
      (Fig.1)

1 馬鈴薯去皮切成極薄圓片(圖2)，放入含鹽1小匙的水中浸泡10分鐘後取出拍乾。

2 將肉塊與①料混合煮至肉熟且汁變濃稠備用。

3 油1杯燒熱，以中火炸馬鈴薯片至酥脆，撈起備用。

4 餘油¼杯炒香洋蔥至微黃，先入②料略拌，續入肉塊煎至色呈金黃、有肉香後取出，置馬鈴薯片上即成。

1 Peel and cut the potatoes into very thin round slices (Fig. 2). Drop them in water with 1 t. salt for 10 minutes. Remove and pat dry.

2 Mix ① with meat and cook until well done and the gravy is thick.

3 Heat 1 c. oil and deep-fry the potatoes over medium heat until crisp; remove and set aside.

4 In ¼ c. of remaining oil fry the onions until lightly brown. Add ② and mix, then add the cooked meat and saute until it is well roasted. Serve with the fried potatoes.

1

2

印度炸肉丸

Fried Indian Meat Balls (Meat Kofta)

瘦絞肉 …………6兩(225公克)

① 蛋 ……………………………1個
麵包粉*或新鮮吐司撕碎(圖1)
……………………………3/4 杯
洋蔥(切碎)、香菜末 …各 1/2 杯
薑末、蒜末 ………各1大匙
小茴香粉 ……………1小匙
胡椒粉、鹽 ………各 1/2 小匙
豆蔻粉 ………………1/4 小匙

1/2 lb. (225g) lean ground
meat (any kind)

① 1 egg
3/4 c. bread crumbs* or a
slice of fresh bread
shredded (Fig. 1)
1/2 c. ea. (chopped): onions,
coriander leaves
1 T. ea. (chopped): garlic,
ginger
1 t. cumin powder
1/2 t. ea.: pepper powder,
salt
1/4 t. nutmeg powder

1 將瘦絞肉加 ① 料拌勻製成22個丸子(圖2)。

2 油1杯燒熱,放入肉丸以中火炸至呈金黃色取出,趁熱以牙籤取用。為一道開胃菜。

＊ 如用乾麵包粉,宜先撒少許水使稍變軟,再與①料拌勻使用。

1 Combine ① and add to meat. Mix thoroughly and make **22** smooth balls (Fig. **2**).

2 Heat 1 c. oil and deep-fry the balls over medium heat until brown. Remove and serve hot with tooth pick in each as an appetizer.

＊ If dry bread crumbs are used, sprinkle a little water first to soften, then mix with ①.

1

2

炸肉餅
Meat Cutlets

瘦絞肉(豬或牛) 6兩(225公克)
熟馬鈴薯泥……6兩(225公克)

① 洋蔥(切碎) ………………1杯
　 紅辣椒末、薑末 ………1大匙

② 番茄醬、鹽 …………各1小匙

③ 蛋黃 …………………………1個
　 茴香粉、小豆蔻粉 …各1大匙
　 肉桂粉、胡椒粉、丁香粉
　 ………………………各 ½ 小匙

蛋白 ………………………1個
麵包粉…………………………適量

½ lb. (225g) ground lean
　meat (pork or beef)
½ lb.(225g) boiled and
　mashed potatoes

① 1 c. chopped onions
　 1 T. ea. (chopped): red chili,
　 ginger

② 1 t. ea.: tomato sauce, salt

③ 1 egg yolk
　 1 T. ea.: fennel powder,
　　cardamom powder
　 ½ t. ea. (powder):
　　cinnamon, pepper, clove

1 egg white
bread crumbs for coating

1　油3大匙燒熱，炒香 ① 料，隨入絞肉及 ② 料，以小火翻炒3分鐘後取出。

2　加 ③ 料及馬鈴薯泥拌勻後，分做成厚1公分，直徑4公分的圓形肉餅(圖1)。

3　蛋白打至起泡(圖2)，將每片肉餅先沾蛋白，再沾裹麵包粉，入熱油1½杯中以中火炸至兩面呈金黃色即成，趁熱與檸檬片及洋蔥圈配食。

1　Heat 3 T. oil and fry ① until fragrant. Add meat and ②. Stir and cook over low heat for **3** minutes; then remove.

2　Add ③ and potatoes; mix well and make a smooth ball. Divide into small portions to make disks of ½" (1cm) thin and 1½" (4cm) in diameter (Fig. 1).

3　Beat the egg white until frothy (Fig. 2). Dip each disk in frothy egg white then in bread crumbs, set aside. Heat 1½ c. oil and deep-fry over medium heat until both sides turn golden brown. Serve hot with lemon wedges and onion rings.

1

2

香辣炒肉塊

Spicy Pork (Pork Masala)

瘦肉塊(圖1) …12兩(450公克)

□1
胡荽粉、醋或優格 …各1大匙
鹽 ………………………1小匙
辣椒粉、小茴香粉、小豆蔻粉
、肉桂粉 ………各 ½ 小匙
鬱金香粉、胡椒粉…各 ¼ 小匙

□2
洋蔥(切片,圖2) ………½杯
薑(切片,圖2) ………1大匙
蒜(切片,圖2) ………1小匙

醋 …………………… ¼杯
香菜末 ……………… ½杯

1 lb. (450g) lean meat
pieces (Fig. 1)

□1
1 T. ea.: coriander powder,
vinegar or yogurt
1 t. salt
½ t. ea. (powder): chili,
cumin, cardamom
cinnamon
¼ t. ea. (powder): turmeric,
pepper

□2
½ c. sliced onions (Fig.2)
1 T. sliced ginger (Fig.2)
1 t. sliced garlic (Fig.2)

¼ c. vinegar
½ c. chopped coriander
leaves

1 將瘦肉塊加 □1 料醃3-4小時。

2 油4大匙燒熱,炒香 □2 料,倒入醃肉及醃汁,並加醋¼杯炒約3分鐘。

3 再加熱水2杯,以中火蓋鍋煮至汁收乾且肉熟軟,撒上香菜拌勻,趁熱食用。

1 Mix and marinate meat in □1 for about 3-4 hours.

2 Heat 4 T. oil and saute □2 until fragrant. Add the meat with the
marinade. Then add ¼ c. vinegar and stir-fry for 3 minutes.

3 Add 2 c. hot water and cook covered over medium heat until
dry and tender. Add coriander leaves and mix well; serve hot.

1

2

馬鈴薯炒肉末
Pork and Potatoes

瘦絞肉 …………8兩(300公克)
馬鈴薯(切1公分塊，圖1) ……
…………6兩(225公克)

☐1 | 洋蔥(切碎) ………………½杯
　　| 蒜末、薑末 …………各1大匙

☐2 | 胡荽粉 …………………1大匙
　　| 辣椒粉、小茴香粉、茴香粉…
　　| …………………各½小匙
　　| 鬱金香粉 ……………¼小匙

☐3 | 番茄(切丁) ………………1杯
　　| 水 ……………………½杯
　　| 鹽 ……………………1小匙
　　| 醋 ……………………½小匙

☐4 | 肉桂粉、小豆蔻粉、胡椒粉…
　　| …………………各½小匙

⅔ lb.(300g) ground lean
　pork
½ lb.(225g) potatoes, cut in
　½" (1cm) cubes (Fig.1)

☐1 | ½ c. chopped onions
　　| 1 T. ea. (chopped): garlic,
　　| ginger

☐2 | 1 T. coriander powder
　　| ½ t. ea. (powder): chili,
　　| cumin, fennel
　　| ¼ t. turmeric powder

☐3 | 1 c. chopped tomatoes
　　| ½ c. water
　　| 1 t. salt
　　| ½ t. vinegar

☐4 | ½ t. ea. (powder):
　　| cinnamon, cardamom,
　　| pepper

1 油4大匙燒熱，炒香 ☐1 料，火轉小，入 ☐2 料略炒，加 ☐3 料拌勻炒1分鐘。

2 入絞肉及馬鈴薯拌炒1分鐘，加水2杯蓋鍋以中火煮至汁收乾且馬鈴薯熟軟，煮時須翻拌，最後撒上 ☐4 料拌勻，趁熱食用。

1 Heat **4** T. oil and saute ☐1. Lower heat; add ☐2 and mix.　Add ☐3 and mix well, and cook for a minute.

2 Add the meat and potatoes. Stir-fry for a minute. Add **2** c. water and cook covered over medium heat until dry and potatoes are done; stir occasionally. Add ☐4, mix well and serve hot.

1

咖哩絞肉

Ground Meat Curry (Meat Kurma)

瘦絞肉(羊或豬肉) ··············
·············8兩(300公克)
洋蔥(切碎) ················1杯

① 薑泥 ····················1大匙
蒜泥 ····················1小匙

② 胡荽粉 ·················2大匙
辣椒粉 ·················1小匙
小茴香粉 ··············1/2 小匙
鬱金香粉 ··············1/4 小匙

③ 番茄(切小丁) ··············1杯
鹽 ·····················1小匙
水 ·····················1/2 杯

④ 小豆蔻粉、丁香粉、肉桂粉···
·····················各 1/2 小匙

2/3 lb. (300g) ground lean
  meat (lamb or pork)
1 c. chopped onions

① 1 T. ginger paste
1 t. garlic paste

② 2 T. coriander powder
1 t. chili powder
1/2 t. cumin powder
1/4 t. turmeric powder

③ 1 c. chopped tomatoes
1 t. salt
1/2 c. water

④ 1/2 t. ea. (powder):
  cardamoms, cloves,
  cinnamon

1 油1/2杯燒熱，炒洋蔥至微黃，隨入 ① 料炒香。

2 火轉小，入 ② 料拌勻，再加 ③ 料拌炒1分鐘成泥狀後，續入絞肉及水
1 1/2杯拌炒並煮5-7分鐘至汁濃稠，撒上 ④ 料拌勻，以香菜裝飾，可趁熱
拌麵或拌飯食用。

1 Heat 1/2 c. oil and fry the onions until light brown. Add ① and
saute until fragrant.

2 Lower heat and add ② and mix well. Add ③ and cook for a
minute. Stir well to form a pulp, then add the meat with 1 1/2 c.
water, mix and cook for 5-7 minutes until the gravy is thick. Add
④, mix well and garnish with coriander leaves. Serve hot with
noodles or rice.

什錦羊肉

Lamb, Lentils and Vegetables (Dhansak)

綠豆仁　………………½ 杯
瘦羊肉塊(圖1)…6兩(225公克)

1 | 洋蔥、番茄(均切丁)　…各1杯
　 南瓜、莆瓜、青椒(均切 2½
　 公分長塊,圖2)* …………
　 ……………共8兩(300公克)

2 | 蒜、薑(均切薄片) …各2大匙

3 | 胡荽粉 ………………2大匙
　 茴香粉 ………………1大匙
　 小茴香粉 ……………1½ 小匙
　 辣椒粉 ………………1小匙
　 鬱金香粉 ……………½ 小匙

4 | 香菜末、蔥末 ……各½ 杯
　 肉桂粉、小豆蔻粉 …各1小匙

½ c. skinless mung beans
　(or any kind of split peas)
½ lb. (225g) fatless lamb
　pieces (Fig.1)

1 | 1 c. ea. (chopped): onions,
　 tomatoes
　 ⅔ lb. (300g): mixed
　 vegetables: pumpkin,
　 bottle gourd, green
　 pepper; all cut in 1" (2½
　 cm) pieces (Fig. 2)*

2 | 2 T. ea. (thinly sliced): garlic,
　 ginger

3 | 2 T. coriander powder
　 1 T. fennel powder
　 1½ t. cumin powder
　 1 t. chili powder
　 ½ t. turmeric powder

4 | ½ c. ea. (chopped):
　 coriander leaves, green
　 onions
　 1 t. ea. (powder):
　 cinnamon, cardamom

1 綠豆仁泡水2小時後瀝乾,與羊肉塊及水3杯以中火蓋鍋煮25分鐘。

2 加 1 料、水1½ 杯及鹽1½ 小匙蓋鍋續煮5-8分鐘至蔬菜熟軟備用,須不時攪拌。

3 油5大匙燒熱,炒香 2 料,火轉小,入 3 料拌勻後,倒入煮過的羊肉、綠豆仁及 4 料再炒勻即成,與米飯配食佳。

* 可依個人喜好加入馬鈴薯或其他蔬菜。

1 Soak mung beans for 2 hours, drain. Then cook covered over medium heat with meat and 3 c. water for 25 minutes.

2 Add 1, 1½ c. water and 1½ t. salt. Cook covered for another 5-8 minutes until the vegetables are done. Stir and set aside.

3 Heat 5 T. oil and fry 2 until fragrant. Lower heat and add 3, stir well and add the cooked items. Add 4 and stir until well blended. Goes well with rice.

* Potato also can be added.

1

2

辣味羊肉

Spicy Lamb

瘦羊肉塊(見65頁) ⋯⋯⋯⋯⋯
⋯⋯⋯⋯⋯⋯12兩(450公克)

1
優格 ⋯⋯⋯⋯⋯⋯⋯⋯½杯
薑泥 ⋯⋯⋯⋯⋯⋯⋯1大匙
鹽 ⋯⋯⋯⋯⋯⋯⋯1¼小匙
胡椒粉、鬱金香粉 各½小匙

2
熱水 ⋯⋯⋯⋯⋯⋯⋯⋯3杯
香菜末 ⋯⋯⋯⋯⋯⋯½杯

3
丁香、小豆蔻(均磨粉) 各5粒
肉桂粉、茴香粉 ⋯各½小匙
豆蔻粉 ⋯⋯⋯⋯⋯¼小匙

1 lb.(450g) boneless lean
  lamb pieces (see p. 65)

1
½ c. yogurt
1 T. ginger paste
1¼ t. salt
½ t. ea. (powder): pepper,
  turmeric

2
3 c. hot water
½ c. chopped coriander
  leaves

3
5 ea. (powder): cloves,
  cardamoms
½ t. ea. (powder) :
  cinnamon, fennel
¼ t. nutmeg powder

1 羊肉以 ① 料醃1小時以上。

2 油4大匙燒熱,入羊肉拌炒2分鐘,續入 ② 料蓋鍋以中火煮40分鐘至肉熟軟,撒上 ③ 料拌勻,趁熱食用。

1 Marinate lamb in ① for at least an hour.

2 Heat 4 T. oil and stir-fry the meat for 2 minutes. Add ② and cook covered over medium heat for about 40 minutes until tender. Add ③, mix well and serve hot.

馬鈴薯羊肉

Lamb and Potatoes

瘦羊肉塊(見65頁) ⋯⋯⋯⋯⋯
⋯⋯⋯⋯⋯8兩(300公克)
馬鈴薯(切2½公分塊) ⋯⋯⋯
⋯⋯⋯⋯⋯4兩(150公克)
洋 蔥(切大丁) ⋯⋯⋯½ 杯

1. 胡荽粉 ⋯⋯⋯⋯⋯⋯⋯1大匙
蒜泥、薑泥 ⋯⋯⋯各½ 大匙
小茴香粉 ⋯⋯⋯⋯⋯⋯1小匙
辣椒粉 ⋯⋯⋯⋯⋯⋯⋯½ 小匙
鬱金粉 ⋯⋯⋯⋯⋯⋯⋯¼ 小匙

2. 優格 ⋯⋯⋯⋯⋯⋯⋯½ 杯
鹽 ⋯⋯⋯⋯⋯⋯⋯1¼ 小匙

3. 小豆蔻粉、茴香粉、肉桂粉、
丁香粉 ⋯⋯⋯⋯各1小匙

⅔ lb (300g) lean lamb
pieces (see p. 65)
⅓ lb (150g) potatoes, cut in
1" (2½ cm) cubes
½ c. chopped onions

1. 1 T. coriander powder
½ T. ea. (paste): garlic,
ginger
1 t. cumin powder
½ t. chili powder
¼ t. turmeric powder

2. ½ c. yogurt
1¼ t. salt

3. 1 t. ea. (powder) :
cardamom, fennel,
cinnamon, cloves

1　油4大匙燒熱,將洋蔥炒至微黃。入 1 料拌勻,隨入羊肉拌炒3-4分鐘。

2　續入 2 料、馬鈴薯及熱水4杯,以中火蓋鍋續煮1小時至肉熟軟。撒上 3
料拌勻,趁熱食用。

1　Heat 4 T oil and fry onions until light brown. Add 1 and mix well.
Add the meat and saute for 3-4 minutes.

2　Add 2, the potatoes and 4 c. hot water then cook covered over
medium heat for 1 hour until the meat is tender. Add 3, mix well
and serve hot.

羊肉香腸
Fried Lamb Sausages

羊瘦絞肉 ⋯⋯⋯6兩(225公克)	
1	蛋黃 ⋯⋯⋯⋯⋯⋯⋯⋯⋯1個 洋蔥末 ⋯⋯⋯⋯⋯⋯⋯½杯 胡荽粉、薑末 ⋯⋯各1大匙 醋、紅辣椒末、肉桂粉⋯⋯⋯ ⋯⋯⋯⋯⋯⋯⋯各1小匙 鹽、胡椒粉、小豆蔻粉、 茴香粉 ⋯⋯⋯⋯各½小匙 土司(撕碎,見60頁) ⋯⋯2片
麵粉 ⋯⋯⋯⋯⋯⋯⋯⋯⋯½杯	

½ lb. (225g) ground lean lamb

1 — 1 egg yolk
½ c. chopped onions
1 T. ea.: coriander powder, chopped ginger
1 t. ea.: vinegar, chopped red chilies, cinnamon powder
½ t. ea.: salt, pepper powder, cardamom powder, fennel powder
2 slices of bread shredded (see p.60)

½ c. flour for coating

1 將 ① 料及肉拌勻分成12份,每份做成長5公分直徑2公分的香腸(圖1)。

2 將麵粉撒在平底盤上,使每一根香腸均勻裹上一層薄麵粉(圖2)。

3 油1½杯燒熱,分批放入香腸炸至兩面呈金黃色(須不時的翻轉)取出,置紙巾上吸乾油後,趁熱與番茄片及檸檬片排盤或用長針串起食用。

1 Combine ① with meat and mix well. Divide into 12 portions and shape each to form a sausage, 2" (5cm) long and ¾" (2cm) in diameter (Fig. 1).

2 Spread the flour over a flat surface. Roll each sausage in flour and smooth the surface (Fig. 2).

3 Heat 1½ c. oil in a flat skillet. Add a few sausages at a time; rotate well until all sides are equally brown. Drain on paper towels. Arrange on skewers with tomato slices and lemon wedges. Serve hot.

1

2

咖哩牛肉

Spicy Beef Curry

瘦牛肉塊 ……12兩(450公克)
芥茉子 ………………1小匙
洋蔥(切片) ……………1⁄2 杯
蒜泥、薑泥 …………各1大匙

1 胡荽粉 ………………2大匙
  辣椒粉、茴香粉 ……各1小匙
  胡椒粉 ………………1⁄2 小匙
  鬱金香粉 ……………1⁄4 小匙

2 醋 …………………………1大匙
  鹽 …………………………1½ 小匙

3 肉桂粉、小豆蔻粉…各 1⁄2 小匙

  椰奶(見38頁)……………1⁄2 杯

1 lb. (450g) thin beef pieces
1 t. mustard seeds
1⁄2 c. sliced onions
1 T. ea. (paste):garlic ,
  ginger

1
  2 T. coriander powder
  1 t. ea. (powder) : chili,
    fennel
  1⁄2 t. pepper powder
  1⁄4 t. turmeric powder

2
  1 T. vinegar
  1½ t. salt

3
  1⁄2 t. ea. (powder):
    cinnamon, cardamom

  1⁄2 c. coconut milk (see p.
  38)

1 油5大匙燒熱,炒芥茉子至爆裂,續入洋蔥炒至微黃,再加蒜、薑泥炒香,火轉小,入 1 料及 2 料拌勻。

2 加入牛肉及熱水3杯煮至肉熟軟,撒上 3 料拌勻,再加椰奶煮1分鐘即成,趁熱食用。

1 Heat 5 T. oil and add the mustard seeds. When they sputter, add onions and stir until slightly brown. Add garlic paste, ginger paste and fry until fragrant. Lower heat; add 1, 2 and stir until well mixed.

2 Add the meat and 3 c. hot water and cook until done. Add 3 and mix. Then add the coconut milk and simmer for a minute. Serve hot.

烘蛋

Egg Roast

水煮蛋(蛋黃煮熟) ……… 4個
洋蔥(切片) ……………… 1杯

1 | 胡荽粉 ………………… 1大匙
　 | 辣椒粉、胡椒粉 …… 各1小匙

2 | 醋 …………………… 1大匙
　 | 鹽 ………………… ½小匙

4 hard boiled eggs
1 c. sliced onions

1 | 1 T. coriander powder
　 | 1 t. ea. (powder): chili,
　 | pepper

2 | 1 T. vinegar
　 | ½ t. salt

1　油4大匙燒熱，將蛋表面煎呈金黃色，撈起縱切半(圖1)備用。

2　餘油炒香洋蔥，火轉小，入 1 料拌炒後續入 2 料拌勻，將蛋放入略拌炒，使蛋均勻裹上辛香料。

3　將蛋切面朝上排盤，上置炒過之洋蔥，並以香菜裝飾，趁熱食用。

1　Heat **4** T. oil and saute the eggs until they become light brown. Remove from oil and cut each egg lengthwise into half (Fig. 1) and set aside.

2　In remaining oil saute onions. Lower heat; add 1, stir then add 2. Add the egg pieces, stir and coat with the fried spices.

3　Arrange the eggs with cut side up on a serving dish. Pour the onion gravy over the eggs. Garnish with coriander leaves and serve hot.

1

咖哩蛋捲

Egg Roll Curry

① 蛋 4個
　 鹽 ....⅛小匙

② 洋蔥(切片) ....½杯
　 薑、蒜(均切片)、辣椒末、
　 　茴香子(略磨) 各1小匙

③ 胡荽粉 1大匙
　 鬱金香粉、胡椒粉、小豆蔻粉
　 、肉桂粉 ....各¼小匙

④ 醋 1大匙
　 鹽 ....½小匙
　 水 ....¾杯

　 椰奶(見38頁)...........½杯

① 4 eggs
　 ⅛ t. salt

② ½ c. sliced onions
　 1 t. ea.: sliced ginger, sliced
　 garlic, chopped chilies,
　 coarsely ground fennel
　 seeds

③ 1 T. coriander powder
　 ¼ t. ea. (powder): turmeric,
　 pepper cardamom,
　 cinnamon

④ 1 T. vinegar
　 ½ t. salt
　 ¾ c. water

　 ½ c. coconut milk (see p.38)

1　將 ① 料打至起泡備用。平底鍋燒熱,抹上油1大匙,先倒入 ½ 的蛋液,均勻鋪開(圖1)煎至熟,捲起成蛋捲(圖2),餘 ½ 的蛋液依此法煎成蛋捲。將煎好之蛋捲切成3公分塊備用。

2　油2大匙燒熱,炒香 ② 料至洋蔥變色,火轉小,入 ③ 料拌勻,再加④ 料略煮,最後倒入蛋捲續煮1分鐘至汁濃稠,淋入椰奶再煮1分鐘,趁熱食用。

1　Beat ① until forthy and set aside. Heat a flat skillet and brush 1 T. oil. Pour in ½ of the egg mixture, spread uniformly and cook until set (Fig. 1). Roll carefully from one end to the other (Fig. 2). Repeat with the remaining egg mixture. Place two rolls together and cut in 1¼" (3cm) pieces.

2　Heat 2 T. oil and saute ② until onions change color. Lower heat and add ③, mix well. Add ④; simmer and add the rolls carefully. Cook for a minute until the gravy thickens. Add coconut milk and cook for a minute. Serve hot.

1

2

素食餃

Vegetarian Rolls (Samosa)

1 | 麵粉 …………………1¼杯
  | 奶油 …………………1大匙
  | 鹽 …………………¼小匙

2 | 洋蔥(切碎) …………1大匙
  | 薑末 …………………½大匙

3 | 胡荽粉 ………………1小匙
  | 茴香粉、小茴香粉、胡椒粉、
  | 辣椒粉 …………各½小匙
  | 鬱金香粉 ……………¼小匙

4 | 熟馬鈴薯(切1公分塊) ……1杯
  | 熟豌豆 ………………½杯
  | 香菜末 ………………¼杯
  | 檸檬汁 ………………1大匙
  | 鹽 …………………½小匙

1 | 1¼ c. flour
  | 1 T. butter
  | ¼ t. salt

2 | 1 T. chopped onions
  | ½ T. chopped ginger

3 | 1 t. coriander powder
  | ½ t. ea. (powder): fennel,
  | cumin, pepper, chili
  | ¼ t. turmeric powder

4 | 1 c. boiled potatoes, cut into
  | ½" (1cm) cubes
  | ½ c. boiled peas
  | ¼ c. chopped coriander
  | leaves
  | 1 T. lemon juice
  | ½ t. salt

1 混合 1 料，加溫水¼杯揉成麵糰，加蓋置旁1小時。

2 油2大匙燒熱，炒香 2 料，火轉小，入 3 料拌炒，再加 4 料炒勻即為餡備用。

3 將麵糰分製成8個直徑12公分的圓餅，每張圓餅從中切成半圓，再捲成圓錐狀，填入內餡(圖1)，開口及邊緣用水黏起(圖2)。

4 油1½杯燒熱，將素食餃以中火炸呈金黃色且酥脆取出，趁熱沾香菜醬(見9頁)食用。

1 Combine 1 and knead well with ¼ c. warm water to form a smooth dough. Cover and set aside for an hour.

2 Heat 2 T. oil and saute 2 until fragrant. Lower heat, add 3 and stir. Add 4, mix well and set aside.

3 Divide the dough to **8** portions and roll each one into a round disk about 4¾" (12cm) in diameter. Cut each in half across the diameter. Form each piece into a cone. Fill the cone with prepared mixture (Fig. 1). Seal the side and top edges with water (Fig. 2).

4 Heat 1½ c.oil and deep-fry samosas over medium heat until golden brown and crisp. Serve hot with coriander sauce (see p. 9).

1

2

印度咖哩餃
Meat Puffs

① 麵粉··················1½杯
　鹽 ····················½小匙
　泡打粉 ··············¼小匙

奶油(融化)············¼杯
蛋(打散) ·············1個
內餡參照馬鈴薯炒肉末(見63
頁)之做法。

① 1½ c. flour
　½ t. salt
　¼ t. baking powder

¼ c. melted butter
1 beaten egg
prepare pork and potatoes
for the filling (see p. 63)

1 ①料先加融化的奶油拌勻，續加蛋液及水2-3大匙揉成麵糰，置旁1小時備用。

2 將麵糰分成12個圓球並趕成直徑8公分的圓餅。

3 每張圓餅包入1大匙內餡並對折成半圓，邊緣用水黏起，以叉子(圖1)或切割器(圖2)在邊緣壓花裝飾，同法將其餘之麵餅做完。

4 油1½杯燒熱，以中火炸麵餅至呈金黃色，可與香菜醬（見9頁）或市售番茄醬配食。

1 Mix ① together, add melted butter and rub into the mixture. Add egg and knead with 2-3 T. water to form a dough. Set aside for an hour.

2 Divide the dough into 12 balls. Roll out each one into a thin disk 3" (8cm) in diameter.

3 Place 1 T. filling in the center and fold over to make a semicircle. Seal the round edge with water. Decorate with a fork (Fig. 1) or a cutter (Fig.2). Repeat the same with the remainder.

4 Heat 1½ c. oil and deep-fry the puffs over medium heat until golden brown. Serve with coriander sauce (see. p. 9) or tomato ketchup.

1

2

炸菠菜丸子

Fried Spinach Balls

菠菜 ‧‧‧‧‧‧‧‧‧‧‧‧‧‧6兩(225公克)

1 ⎰ 洋蔥(切碎) ‧‧‧‧‧‧‧‧‧‧‧‧‧‧‧‧‧½杯
⎱ 辣椒粉、鹽 ‧‧‧‧‧‧‧‧各½小匙
⎱ 酥炸粉 ‧‧‧‧‧‧‧‧‧‧‧‧‧‧‧‧‧‧‧5大匙

½ lb. (225g) spinach

1 ⎰ ½ c. chopped onions
⎱ ½ t. ea.: chili powder, salt
⎱ 5 T. fryer mix powder

1 菠菜洗淨瀝乾，切碎後調入 1 料拌勻，分別做成12個小丸子備用。

2 油1½杯燒熱，將菠菜丸子炸至呈金黃色，與茶配食佳。

1 Wash, drain and finely chop spinach. Add 1 and mix well. Divide into 12 portions and make small balls.

2 Heat 1½ c. oil and deep-fry spinach balls until golden brown. Goes well with tea.

炸洋蔥球

Fried Onion Balls (Onion Fritters)

洋蔥(切碎) ⋯⋯⋯⋯⋯1杯

|1| 麵粉 ⋯⋯⋯⋯⋯⋯5大匙
水 ⋯⋯⋯⋯⋯⋯2大匙
鹽、辣椒粉 ⋯⋯各 1/2 小匙
鬱金香粉、小茴香粉各 1/4 小匙
小蘇打粉 ⋯⋯⋯⋯ 1/8 小匙

1 c. chopped onions

|1| 5 T. flour
2 T. water
1/2 t. ea.: salt, chili powder
1/4 t. ea. (powder): turmeric,
  cumin
1/8 t. baking soda

1 將切好的洋蔥與 |1| 料調勻製成麵糊。

2 油1 1/2杯燒熱,將麵糊一匙一匙地舀入鍋中,以中火炸至呈金黃色即成。
趁熱與番茄醬(見9頁)配食,為極佳的茶點。

1 Combine the onions and |1| to form a thick batter.

2 Heat 1 1/2 c. oil and drop in spoonfuls of the batter. Fry over
medium heat until golden brown. Serve hot with any tomato
sauce or chutney (see p. 9) as a good tea time snack.

油炸什錦蔬菜
Deep-Fried Mixed Vegetables (Pakodas)

馬鈴薯、茄子、洋蔥、青椒…
…………共6兩(225公克)

① 麵粉、再來米粉(圖1) ………
…………各1／3杯
辣椒粉 …………3／4 小匙
小蘇打粉、鹽、小茴香子……
…………各 1/2 小匙

½ lb. (225g) mixed
vegetables: potatoes,
eggplant, onions, green
peppers

① ⅓ c. ea.: flour, non-sticky
rice powder (Fig.1)
¾ t. chili powder
½ t. ea.: baking soda, salt,
cumin seeds

1 蔬菜洗淨並切0.4公分圓薄片(圖2)備用。

2 ① 料拌勻並緩緩加水 ½ 杯攪拌成麵糊。

3 油2杯燒熱,將蔬菜片沾麵糊(圖3)後放入油中,以中火炸至呈金黃色。趁熱沾香菜醬(見9頁)或任何辣醬食用,是極佳的午茶點心。

1 Wash and cut the vegetables into ⅛" (0.4cm) thin round slices (Fig. 2) and set aside.

2 Mix ① thoroughly and add ½ c. water gradually to form a batter.

3 Heat 2 c. oil in a wok. Dip each piece of vegetable in the batter (Fig. 3) and deep-fry until golden brown. Serve hot with coriander sauce (see p. 9) or any hot sauce. A good tea time snack.

1

2

3

炸馬鈴薯球

Deep-Fried Potato Balls (Bonda)

熟馬鈴薯泥 ……8兩(300公克)

1 | 芥茉子、小茴香子 各½小匙

2 | 洋蔥(切碎) ………………½ 杯
　 薑末、紅辣椒末 ……各1小匙

3 | 檸檬汁 …………………1小匙
　 鹽 ………………………¾小匙
　 鬱金香粉 ………………¼小匙

4 | 麵粉 ……………………½ 杯
　 鹽、小蘇打粉 ……各¼小匙
　 水 ……………………6大匙

⅔ lb. (300g) boiled and
mashed potatoes

1 | ½ t. ea.: mustard seeds,
　 cumin seeds

2 | ½ c. chopped onions
　 1 t. ea. (chopped): ginger,
　 red chilies

3 | 1 t. lemon juice
　 ¾ t. salt
　 ¼ t. turmeric powder

4 | ½ c. flour
　 ¼ t. ea.: salt, baking soda
　 6 T. water

1 油2大匙燒熱，先炒 1 料至爆裂，再入 2 料炒至微黃。

2 火轉小，續入 3 料及馬鈴薯泥拌勻，分成15個薯球備用。

3 將 4 料調勻製成麵糊。油1½杯燒熱，將馬鈴薯球均勻沾上麵糊後，每次2-3個入油中以中火炸至呈金黃色，趁熱與椰子醬(見10頁)或香菜醬(見9頁)配食。

1 Heat 2 T. oil and add 1. After they sputter, add 2 and saute until slightly brown.

2 Lower heat; add 3, potatoes and mix well. Make 15 smooth balls with the mixture. Set aside.

3 Mix 4 thoroughly and make a batter. Heat 1½ c. oil; dip each ball in the batter and deep-fry 2 or 3 at a time over medium heat until golden brown. Serve hot with coconut sauce (see p. 10) or coriander sauce (see p. 9).

馬鈴薯餅

Potato Patties

熟馬鈴薯泥 ……8兩(300公克)
吐司麵包 ………………2片

1 | 洋蔥(切碎) ……………½杯
   紅辣椒末、薑末 ……各1小匙

炸油 ………………………½杯

⅔ lb. (300g) boiled and
  mashed potatoes
2 slices of fresh bread

1 | ½ c. chopped onions
   1 t. ea.(chopped): red
     chilies, ginger

½ c. oil for shallow frying

1 將麵包泡水至軟，擠乾水份(圖1)加入馬鈴薯泥中拌勻。

2 油1大匙燒熱，炒香 1 料，與鹽 ½ 小匙一起加入馬鈴薯泥中拌勻，分成8份並分別做成1公分厚之任何形狀薯餅。

3 平底鍋入炸油燒熱，將薯餅以小火煎至兩面呈金黃色，趁熱與香菜醬(見9頁)配食。

1 Dip the bread in water until soft; squeeze out water (Fig.1) and mix with the potatoes.

2 Heat 1 T. oil and saute 1 until fragrant. Add ½ t. salt, the potato mixture and combine well. Divide into **8** portions and make smooth patties in any shape, ½" (1cm) thick.

3 Heat the oil and place the patties in a flat skillet. Fry over low heat until both sides are golden brown. Serve hot with coriander sauce (see p. 9).

1

什錦蔬菜煎餅

Mixed Vegetable Cutlets

熟馬鈴薯泥 ·················1杯

1 包心菜、紅蘿蔔、四季豆、白
花菜、豌豆(均切絲) 共2杯

2 洋蔥(切丁)···············½杯
薑末、紅辣椒末 ······各1小匙

3 香菜末 ·················2大匙
檸檬汁 ·················2小匙
鹽 ·····················1小匙
黑胡椒粉 ··············½小匙

麵粉 ···················1大匙

4 麵粉 ···················5大匙
水 ·····················6大匙

麵包粉··················適量

1 c. boiled and mashed
potatoes

1 2 c. shredded vegetables:
cabbage,carrot, French
beans, cauliflower, peas

2 ½ c. chopped onions
1 t. ea. (chopped): ginger,
red chilies

3 2 T. chopped coriander
leaves
2 t. lemon juice
1 t. salt
½ t. black pepper powder

1 T. flour

4 5 T. flour
6 T. water

bread crumbs for coating

1 ① 料加水½杯煮4-5分鐘至水收乾。

2 油2大匙燒熱，炒香 ② 料約1分鐘，再加煮過的蔬菜炒1分鐘，隨入 ③ 料
及馬鈴薯泥拌勻，再加麵粉1大匙混勻，並做成12個1公分厚的圓餅備
用。

3 ④ 料調勻成麵糊，油1杯燒熱，將蔬菜餅先沾麵糊再均勻裹上麵包粉，入
熱油中以中火炸至兩面呈金黃色即成，趁熱與香菜醬(見9頁)配食。

1 Cook ① with ½ c. water for **4-5** minutes until dry.

2 Heat **2** T. oil and saute ② for a minute. Add the cooked
vegetables and stir for a minute. Add ③ and potatoes. Stir and
add **1** T. flour, mix well. Prepare **12** round cutlets, ½" (1cm) thick.
Set aside.

3 Prepare a batter with ④. Dip each cutlet first in the batter, then
coat evenly with bread crumbs. Heat **1**c.oil and shallow-fry
cutlets over medium heat until both sides turn golden brown.
Serve hot with coriander sauce (see p. 9).

馬鈴薯薄餅
Shredded Potato Pancake

4人份 · Serves 4

馬鈴薯(去皮,切絲)⋯⋯⋯⋯⋯
⋯⋯⋯⋯⋯8兩(300公克)

① 麵粉 ⋯⋯⋯⋯⋯⋯1大匙
胡椒粉、粗粒辣椒粉⋯⋯⋯⋯
⋯⋯⋯⋯各½小匙
鹽 ⋯⋯⋯⋯⋯¼小匙

② 奶油、油 ⋯⋯⋯各2大匙

蔥末 ⋯⋯⋯⋯⋯½杯

⅔ lb. (300g) peeled and
shredded potatoes

① 1 T. flour
½ t. ea.: pepper powder,
red chili flakes
¼ t. salt

② 2 T. ea.: butter, oil

½ c. chopped green onions

1 馬鈴薯絲拌入 ① 料備用。

2 ② 料於平底鍋燒熱,入馬鈴薯絲炒勻,壓平並撒上蔥,再用鍋鏟輕壓使成大張薄餅(圖1)。亦可做成兩張小薄餅。

3 以小火烘烤8-10分鐘至呈金黃色,翻面續烤至熟,切片趁熱與辣醬配食。

1 Mix ① and potatoes well.

2 Heat ② in a flat skillet, add the potato mixture, and stir well. Flatten the mixture uniformly and sprinkle green onions on top. Lightly press down with the spatula to make the surface even (Fig. 1). This can also be made into 2 pancakes.

3 Roast over low heat for 8-10 minutes until golden brown. Turn over and cook until done. Cut into slices and serve hot with any spicy sauce.

1

綠豆薄餅
Mung Bean Pancake

綠豆仁 ‥‥‥‥‥‥‥‥‥1杯

① 薑末、紅辣椒末 ‥‥‥各1小匙
水 ‥‥‥‥‥‥‥‥‥½杯

② 鹽 ‥‥‥‥‥‥‥‥‥1小匙
小蘇打粉 ‥‥‥‥‥¼小匙

③ 洋蔥(切碎) ‥‥‥‥‥½杯
香菜末 ‥‥‥‥‥‥1大匙

洋蔥末 ‥‥‥‥‥‥‥8大匙

1 c. skinless mung beans

① 1 t. ea. (chopped): ginger,
red chilies
½ c. water

② 1 t. salt
¼ t. baking soda

③ ½ c. chopped onions
1 T. chopped coriander
leaves

8 T. finely chopped onions

1 綠豆仁洗淨泡水2小時後瀝乾,加 ① 料用果汁機打成泥,再加 ②、③ 料拌勻備用。

2 平底鍋燒熱,刷上油1小匙,倒入 ⅛ 的綠豆泥並使其均勻散開(圖1), 再撒上洋蔥1大匙並輕壓,煎約1分鐘後翻面續煎至呈金黃色。依法將其餘7個餅煎好,趁熱與辣椒醬或香菜醬(見9頁)配食。

1 Wash and soak the mung beans for 2 hours; drain. Add ① and grind in blender to form a paste. Add ② and ③. Mix well and set aside.

2 Heat a flat skillet and brush with 1 t. oil. Pour ⅛ of the mixture and spread evenly (Fig. 1). Spread 1 T. onions on top and press slightly. Cook for a minute, turn over and cook until golden brown. Make 7 more pancakes. Serve hot with chili sauce or coriander sauce (see p.9).

1

鹹味鑽石餅

Salty Diamond Cuts

麵粉 ……………………1杯
奶油(融化) …………1大匙

① 黑芝麻、小茴香子 …各1小匙
鹽 ………………………½小匙

溫牛奶 …………………¼杯

1 c. flour
1 T. melted butter

① 1 t. ea.: black sesame
    seeds, cumin seeds
½ t. salt

¼ c. warm milk

1 麵粉加奶油混合，入 ① 料拌勻後，緩緩倒入溫牛奶，並揉成堅實的麵糰。

2 將麵糰分成3份，分別趕成直徑18公分之圓薄餅，並切成2公分×4公分之菱形片(圖1)，重複兩次將其餘麵糰製好備用。

3 油1½杯燒熱，將麵餅分批放入炸至呈金黃色且酥脆即成。為午茶極佳的點心。

☐ 所有炸過的香脆點心，待涼後裝入密閉容器內可保存約2-3週。

1 Add butter to the flour and mix well. Add ① and mix well. Then add milk gradually and knead well to make a smooth dough.

2 Divide the dough into 3 parts and roll each into a thin round disk, 7" (18cm) in diameter. Cut into small diamond shaped pieces, 1" x 1¾" (2cm x 4cm) (Fig. 1). Repeat the process with the remainder and set aside.

3 Heat 1 ½ c. oil and deep-fry in small batches until crisp and golden brown. Use as a good tea time snack.

☐ All deep-fried crisp snacks can be stored in airtight containers for 2-3 weeks.

1

綠豆麵球

Deep-Fried Mung Bean Balls (Vada)

綠豆仁 ⋯⋯⋯⋯⋯⋯⋯⋯1杯

1 | 洋蔥(切碎) ⋯⋯⋯⋯1大匙
  | 紅辣椒末、薑末 ⋯⋯各1小匙

2 | 麵粉 ⋯⋯⋯⋯⋯⋯⋯⋯2大匙
  | 鹽 ⋯⋯⋯⋯⋯⋯⋯⋯⋯1小匙

1 c. skinless mung beans

1 | 1 T. chopped onions
  | 1 t. ea. (chopped): red
  | chilies, ginger

2 | 2 T. flour
  | 1 t. salt

1 綠豆仁洗淨泡水2小時後瀝乾，加水3大匙以攪拌機略打攪拌成泥狀(圖1)後，加入 ①、② 料拌勻成稀麵糊。

2 油1½ 杯燒熱，湯匙沾水將麵糊一匙匙舀入熱油中，以中火炸呈金黃色取出並瀝乾油，趁熱與椰子醬(見10頁)配食。

1 Wash and soak the mung beans in water for **2** hours. Drain and blend coarsely with **3** T. water (Fig. 1). Add ①, ② and mix well to form a thick paste.

2 Heat 1½ c. oil; using a wet tablespoon drop the batter in lumps into the hot oil. Fry over medium heat until golden brown. Drain and set aside. Repeat until all the batter is used. Serve hot with coconut sauce (see p. 10).

1

紅糖米球
Brown Sugar Rice Balls

1️⃣ 再來米粉、麵粉、紅糖、
　　椰子粉 ……………各½杯
　　黑芝麻(略烤)、腰果(略敲)、
　　葡萄乾 …………各1大匙
　　小豆蔻粉 …………½小匙
　　小蘇打粉、鹽 ……各¼小匙
　　椰片(圖1) ……1大匙(無亦可)

1️⃣ ½ c. ea.: non-sticky rice
　　powder, flour, brown
　　sugar, coconut flakes
　1 T. ea.: roasted black
　　sesame seeds, crushed
　　nuts, raisins
　½ t. cardamom powder
　¼ t. ea.: baking soda, salt
　1 T. fried coconut chips
　　(optional; Fig.1)

1 將 1️⃣ 料混合，加溫水 ½ 杯拌勻成麵糊。

2 油2杯燒熱，以湯匙先沾熱油以防沾黏，將麵糊一匙匙舀入鍋中，以中火炸至呈金黃色並稍膨起成球狀即成。與茶配食佳。

1 Combine 1️⃣ and mix. Add ½ c.warm water to make a thick batter.

2 Heat 2 c. oil and drop in the batter in lumps using a tablespoon dipped in hot oil to avoid sticking. Fry until golden brown over medium heat. They swell into round balls when done. Serve with tea.

1

甜綠豆球

Sweet Green Gram Balls (Sukhian)

綠豆	⋯⋯⋯⋯⋯½杯

1
紅糖、椰子粉	⋯⋯⋯⋯各1杯
奶油	⋯⋯⋯⋯⋯⋯1大匙
小豆蔻粉	⋯⋯⋯⋯⋯1小匙

2
麵粉	⋯⋯⋯⋯⋯⋯4大匙
再來米粉	⋯⋯⋯⋯2大匙
鹽	⋯⋯⋯⋯⋯⋯⅛小匙
水	⋯⋯⋯⋯⋯⋯¼杯

½ c. whole green gram

1
1 c. ea.: brown sugar,
  coconut flakes
1 T. butter
1 t. cardamom powder

2
4 T. flour
2 T. non-sticky rice powder
⅛ t. salt
¼ c. water

1 綠豆洗淨瀝乾，在乾鍋中烤(圖1)約2分鐘後，加熱水 2½ 杯蓋鍋煮至綠豆熟軟且汁收乾(圖2)。

2 加入 ① 料拌勻，待冷分成16個小球。將 ② 料調勻製成麵糊備用。

3 油1½杯燒熱，將綠豆球沾裹麵糊，以中火炸呈金黃色即成。

1 Wash and drain the green gram, then roast in a dry wok for about 2 minutes (Fig. 1). Then cook covered with 2½ c. hot water until soft and dry (Fig. 2).

2 Add ①, mix and set aside to cool, then divide the mixture into 16 balls. Make a batter with ②; set aside.

3 Heat 1½ c. oil; dip each ball in the batter and deep-fry over medium heat until golden brown.

1

2

炸香蕉餅
Banana Fritters

熟香蕉(大) ················4根

1 ┌ 麵粉、水···············各½杯
  │ 再來米粉···············¼杯
  └ 糖 ···················2大匙

4 large ripe bananas

1 ┌ ½ c. flour and water
  │ ¼ c. non-sticky rice powder
  └ 2 T. sugar

1 香蕉去皮，每根橫切成兩半，每塊再切成3長片(圖1)備用。1 料調勻成麵糊。

2 油1½杯燒熱，將香蕉片均勻沾上麵糊，以中火炸至呈金黃色，撒上冰糖裝飾並趁熱食用。

1 Peel the bananas and cut in two crosswise. Then cut each piece into 3 long slices (Fig. 1); set aside. Mix 1 thoroughly to make a batter.

2 Heat 1½ c. oil; dip each piece in the batter and deep-fry until golden brown. Sprinkle sugar on top for garnishing. Serve hot.

1

香烤香蕉
Banana Bake

熟香蕉(大) ⋯⋯⋯⋯⋯4根
柳橙汁 ⋯⋯⋯⋯⋯⋯⋯1杯

1 　糖 ⋯⋯⋯⋯⋯⋯⋯1/2 杯
　　肉桂粉 ⋯⋯⋯⋯⋯1/2 小匙
　　豆蔻粉 ⋯⋯⋯⋯⋯1/4 小匙

2 　奶油(融化) ⋯⋯⋯⋯1大匙
　　椰子粉 ⋯⋯⋯⋯⋯1大匙

4 large ripe bananas
1 c. orange juice

1 　1/2 c. sugar
　　1/2 t. cinnamon powder
　　1/4 t. nutmeg powder

2 　1 T. melted butter
　　1 T. coconut flakes

1 　香蕉去皮並切成6塊(見86頁)，排於烤盤上。

2 　淋入柳橙汁及撒上混勻之 1 料，最後加 2 料。

3 　烤箱預熱，以375°F(190°C)烤10分鐘即成，以湯匙舀出盛盤，為極佳的點心。可於烘烤前撒上壓碎的腰果及葡萄乾各1大匙，以增加風味。

1 Peel and slice each banana into 6 pieces (see p. 86). Arrange in a baking tray.

2 Pour the orange juice over the bananas. Mix 1 together and sprinkle over the bananas. Finally, add 2.

3 Bake for 10 minutes in a preheated oven at 375°F (190°C). Ladle out and serve as a tasty dessert. For richness and flavor, 1 T. each of crushed nuts and raisins can be spread on top before baking.

甜紅蘿蔔餅

Carrot Sweet (Gajar Halva)

紅蘿蔔(切絲) …8兩(300公克)
全脂牛奶 …………………3杯
糖 ……………………………1杯

1 ｜ 葡萄乾(圖1) ……………½杯
｜ 腰果、杏仁(均略敲碎，圖1)
｜ ……………………………各5粒

奶油(融化)…………………½杯
小豆蔻粉 ………………1小匙

⅔ lb. (300g) shredded
  carrots
3 c. whole milk
1 c. sugar

1 ｜ ½ c. raisins (Fig.1)
｜ 5 ea. (crushed): cashew
｜ nuts, almonds (Fig.1)

½ c. melted butter
1 t. cardamom powder

1 紅蘿蔔加牛奶以中火煮約15分鐘或至牛奶被吸收後，加糖續煮至計收乾，撒上 1 料拌勻。

2 將奶油緩緩倒入攪拌至濃稠成糰且不黏鍋(圖2)，隨入小豆蔻粉拌勻，置於塗油之凹盤中鋪平，待冷後切三角形或方塊食用。

☐ 在印度，上這道甜點時，常會撒上一層可食性的極薄銀紙作為裝飾。

1 Cook the carrots in milk over medium heat for about **15** minutes or until the milk is absorbed. Add sugar, stir and cook until dry. Add 1 and mix.

2 Add butter gradually and stir until the mixture is thick enough to draw away from the sides of the wok (Fig. **2**). Add cardamom and mix well. Transfer to a buttered tray and level the surface. When set, cut in wedges or squares to serve.

☐ In india, this sweet dessert is garnished with very thin edible silver paper.

1

2

甜麥球

Cream of Wheat Balls (Rava Laddoo)

小麥精粉(圖1) ……………1杯
奶油 ……………………¼杯

① 腰果(敲碎) …………1大匙
　 葡萄乾 ………………1大匙

糖粉 ……………………⅔杯
牛奶 ……………………2大匙
小豆蔻粉 ………………1小匙

1 c. cream of wheat (Fig.1)
¼ c. butter

① 1 T. crushed cashew nuts
　 1 T. raisins

⅔ c. sugar powder
2 T. milk
1 t. cardamom powder

1 奶油燒熱，略炒 ① 料取出備用。

2 餘油拌炒小麥精粉1分鐘，保持原色並避免炒焦。

3 加糖粉拌勻，轉小火，依序加入牛奶、小豆蔻粉及炒過的 ① 料拌勻，熄火，趁未冷卻前做成16個小球即成。

1 Heat butter and briefly fry ①, remove and set aside.

2 In the remaining butter, fry and stir the cream of wheat for a minute without changing color.

3 Add sugar powder and stir well. Lower heat and sprinkle the milk; add cardamom powder and the fried ①. Mix well. Turn off the heat and make **16** balls before the mixture turns cold.

1

玫瑰甜球

Milk Powder Balls in Sugar Syrup (Gulab Jamun)

1️⃣
奶粉 ·························1杯
麵粉 ·······················4大匙
小蘇打粉 ··············½小匙

奶油(融化) ·············1大匙
熱牛奶 ·················3-4大匙

2️⃣
糖 ·························¾杯
水 ·························1¼杯
丁香 ·····················3粒
玫瑰精(圖1) ············½小匙

1️⃣
1 c. milk powder
4 T. flour
½ t. baking soda

1 T. melted butter
3-4 T. hot milk

2️⃣
¾ c. sugar
1¼ c. water
3 cloves

½ t. rose essence (Fig.1)

1 將 1️⃣ 料加融化的奶油混合調勻,再緩緩倒入牛奶略搓揉,做成16個小球備用。

2 2️⃣ 料煮沸至糖完全融化,加玫瑰精備用。

3 油1杯燒熱,每次入麵球4-5個以中火炸至呈黃棕色取出,瀝乾油並置熱糖漿中(圖2)浸30分鐘使入味後即成,並以整朵玫瑰或玫瑰花瓣裝飾。

1 Combine 1️⃣, then add melted butter to mix. Add milk gradually; mix together without kneading too much. Make **16** smooth balls and set aside.

2 Boil 2️⃣ until the sugar is dissolved completely. Add rose essence then set aside.

3 Heat **1** c. oil and carefully fry **4-5** balls at a time over medium heat until they turn dark brown. Remove and drain oil. Put them in the hot sugar syrup (Fig. 2). Serve after **30** minutes when balls have absorbed the syrup. Garnish with rose or petals.

1

2

蝴蝶結酥餅

4人份 · Serves 4

Sweet Bows

①	麵粉 ·················· 1杯	
	奶油(融化) ·········· 1大匙	
	鹽 ·················· $\frac{1}{8}$ 小匙	
	水 ·················· $\frac{1}{4}$ 杯	
②	糖 ·················· 3大匙	
	水 ·················· 3 $\frac{1}{2}$ 大匙	
③	食用色素(圖1，顏色任選) 2滴	
	香草粉 ·············· $\frac{1}{2}$ 小匙	

① 1 c. flour
1 T. melted butter
$\frac{1}{8}$ t. salt

$\frac{1}{4}$ c. water

② 3 T. sugar
3 $\frac{1}{2}$ T. water

③ 2 drops of any food color
(Fig.1)
$\frac{1}{2}$ t. vanilla powder

1 ① 料調勻並緩緩加水揉成麵糰，置旁半小時。

2 將麵糰分成2份，分別趕成極薄麵皮，以玻璃杯或切割器切出直徑5公分之圓形麵皮，將麵皮中央部份捏緊成蝴蝶結狀(圖2)。

3 油1 $\frac{1}{2}$ 杯燒熱，入麵皮以中火炸至呈金黃色且酥脆取出。

4 ②、③ 料混合加熱製成糖漿，將炸好的麵皮放入，攪拌至糖漿均勻裹在麵皮上取出，待冷食用。

1 Combine ① and mix well. Add water gradually to make a dough. Set aside for half an hour.

2 Divide the dough in 2 portions and roll out each as thin as possible. Using a glass or cutter, cut out disks about 2" (5cm) in diameter. Press to make gathers or pleats at the center to form a bow shape (Fig. 2).

3 Heat 1$\frac{1}{2}$ c. oil and deep-fry bows over medium heat until brown and crisp.

4 Prepare a syrup by mixing and heating ② and ③. Add in the bows and stir until well coated with syrup; remove. Cool and serve.

1

2

西米露麵線布丁
Sago Noodle Pudding

麵線(淡味，圖1) 1把(50公克)
西谷米 ……………………1/3 杯
奶油 ………………………1大匙

① | 葡萄乾、腰果(略敲) 各2大匙

② | 牛奶 ……………………2杯
　| 糖 ………………………3/4 杯

③ | 小豆蔻粉、香草粉 …各1小匙

2 oz. (50g) unsalted noodles
　(Fig.1)
1/3 c. sago
1 T. butter

① | 2 T. ea.: raisins, crushed
　| cashew nuts

② | 2 c. milk
　| 3/4 c. sugar

③ | 1 t. ea.: cardamom powder,
　| vanilla powder

1 西谷米加水2/3杯浸泡半小時。奶油燒熱，略炒 ① 料後取出備用。

2 將麵線切成5公分長段，用餘油略炒，並保持原色(圖2)。

3 炒好的麵線加西谷米及水2 1/2 杯煮5-8分鐘，續入炒過之 ① 料及 ② 料攪拌煮至呈濃稠狀，再加 ③ 料拌勻即成，冷熱食均可。

1 Soak sago in 2/3 c. water for half an hour. Heat butter and briefly fry ①. Remove and set aside.

2 Break the noodles to 2" (5cm) pieces and roast them in the remaining butter without changing color (Fig. 2).

3 Cook the roasted noodles with sago in 2 1/2 c. water for 5-8 minutes. Then add fried ① and ②; stir and cook until it thickens. Add ③, stir and remove from heat. Serve hot or cold as a good dessert.

1

2

甜味優格
Sweet Yogurt Drink (Lassi)

4杯・Serves 4

①	優格 …………………2杯	① 2 c. yogurt
	糖 …………………6大匙	6 T. sugar
	檸檬汁 ……………2大匙	2 T. lemon juice
	薑粉 ………………2小匙	2 t. ginger powder

1 ①料調勻加水1杯用果汁機打勻。

2 將打好的飲料平均倒入4個玻璃杯中，放入冰塊稍攪拌，並在杯緣放置一片檸檬即可，是適合夏天飲用之清涼飲料。

鹹味優格　用鹽½小匙取代糖，並以薑末、洋蔥末各1大匙取代薑粉即成。

1 Mix ① and blend with 1 c. water.

2 Take 4 tall glasses, pour ¼ of the mixture into each one. Add ice cubes to fill the glass and stir well. Fix a lemon slice on the edge and serve. A cool refreshing drink for summer.

Salty Yogurt Drink　Use ½ t. salt instead of sugar and add 1 T. crushed ginger and 1 T. crushed onions instead of ginger powder.

雪克香蕉牛奶
Banana Milk Shake

4杯・Serves 4

①	熟香蕉(切塊) …………2杯	① 2 c. chopped ripe bananas
	牛奶 ………………2杯	2 c. milk
	糖 …………………6大匙	6 T. sugar

1 ①料調勻，用果汁機打至起泡，平均倒入4個玻璃杯中，加冰塊飲用。

雪克芒果牛奶　將甜芒果汁及牛奶各2杯、糖4大匙，加入檸檬汁4大匙同打至起泡即成，加冰塊飲用。

1 Mix ① and blend until forthy. Serve in 4 tall glasses with ice.

Mango Milk Shake　Use 2 c. sweet mango juice with 2 c. milk and 4 T. sugar. Add 4 T. lemon juice. Blend to form Mango Milk Shake.

薑味檸檬雪碧
Lemon Ginger Sherbet

4杯・Serves 4

①	新鮮檸檬汁……………¾杯	① ¾ c. fresh lemon juice
	水 …………………4杯	4 c. water
	糖…………………¾杯	¾ c. sugar
	薑泥 ………………4小匙	4 t. ginger paste

1 ①料調勻，平均倒入4個杯中，加冰塊至滿，攪拌後馬上飲用。

1 Mix ① thoroughly. Transfer to 4 tall glasses. And add ice to fill. Stir well and serve immediately.

索 引

Index